# SAUNDERS PHYSICAL ACTIVITIES SERIES

**Edited by**

**MARYHELEN VANNIER, Ed.D.**
Professor and Director, Women's Division
Department of Health and Physical Education
Southern Methodist University

**and**

**HOLLIS F. FAIT, Ph.D.**
Professor of Physical Education
School of Physical Education
University of Connecticut

# FOIL FENCING

**WANEEN WYRICK**

Associate Professor
Department of Physical and Health Education
The University of Texas at Austin

ILLUSTRATED BY: GRANT LASHBROOK

W. B. SAUNDERS COMPANY

PHILADELPHIA • LONDON • TORONTO

W. B. Saunders Company: West Washington Square
Philadelphia, Pa. 19105

12 Dyott Street
London WC1A 1DB

833 Oxford Street
Toronto 18, Ontario

Saunders Physical Activities Series

Foil Fencing                                                     SBN 0-7216-9614-7

Print No.    9    8    7    6    5    4    3    2

# EDITORS' FOREWORD

Every period of history, as well as every society, has its own profile. Our own world of the last third of the twentieth century is no different. Whenever we step back to look at ourselves, we can see excellences and failings, strengths and weaknesses, that are peculiarly ours.

One of our strengths as a nation is that we are a sports-loving people. Today more persons — and not just young people — are playing, watching, listening to, and reading about sports and games. Those who enjoy themselves most are the men and women who actually *play* the game: the "doers."

You are reading this book now for either of two very good reasons. First, you want to learn — whether in a class or on your own — how to play a sport well, and you need clear, easy-to-follow instructions to develop the special skills involved. If you want to be a successful player, this book will be of much help to you.

Second, you may already have developed skill in this activity, but want to improve your performance through assessing your weaknesses and correcting your errors. You want to develop further the skills you have now and to learn and perfect additional ones. You realize that you will enjoy the activity even more if you know more about it.

In either case, this book can contribute greatly to your success. It offers "lessons" from a real professional: from an outstandingly successful coach, teacher, or performer. All the authors in the *Saunders Physical Activities Series* are experts and widely recognized in their specialized fields. Some have been members or coaches of teams of national prominence and Olympic fame.

This book, like the others in our Series, has been written to make it easy for you to help yourself to learn. The authors and the editors want you to become more self-motivated and to gain a greater understanding of, appreciation for, and proficiency in the exciting world of *movement*. All the activities described in this Series — sports, games, dance, body conditioning, and weight and figure control activities — require skillful, efficient movement. That's what physical activity is all about. Each book contains descriptions and helpful tips about the nature, value, and purpose of an activity, about the purchase and care of equipment, and about the fundamentals of each movement skill involved. These books also tell you about common errors and how to avoid making them, about ways in which you can improve your performance, and about game rules and strategy, scoring, and special techniques. Above all, they should tell you how to get the most pleasure and benefit from the time you spend.

Our purpose is to make you a successful *participant* in this age of sports activities. If you are successful, you will participate often — and this will give you countless hours of creative and recreative fun. At the same time, you will become more physically fit.

"Physical fitness" is more than just a passing fad or a slogan. It is a condition of your body which determines how effectively you can perform your daily work and play and how well you can meet unexpected demands on your strength, your physical skills, and your endurance. How fit you are depends largely on your participation in vigorous physical activity. Of course no one sports activity can provide the kind of total workout of the body required to achieve optimal fitness; but participation with vigor in any activity makes a significant contribution to this total. Consequently, the activity you will learn through reading this book can be extremely helpful to you in developing and maintaining physical fitness now and throughout the years to come.

These physiological benefits of physical activity are important beyond question. Still, the pure pleasure of participation in physical activity will probably provide your strongest motivation. The activities taught in this Series are *fun*, and they provide a most satisfying kind of recreation for your leisure hours. Also they offer you great personal satisfaction in achieving success in skillful performance — in the realization that you are able to control your body and its movement and to develop its power and beauty. Further, there can be a real sense of fulfillment in besting a skilled opponent or in exceeding a goal you have set for yourself. Even when you fall short of such triumphs, you can still find satisfaction in the effort you have made to meet a challenge. By participating in sports you can gain greater respect for yourself, for others, and for "the rules of the game." Your skills in leadership and fellowship will be sharpened and improved. Last, but hardly least, you will make new friends among others who enjoy sports activities, both as participants and as spectators.

We know you're going to enjoy this book. We hope that it — and the others in our Series — will make you a more skillful and more enthusiastic performer in all the activities you undertake.

Good luck!

MARYHELEN VANNIER

HOLLIS FAIT

# CONTENTS

## Chapter 5

## Chapter 6

## CHAPTER 1

# NATURE AND PURPOSE OF FENCING

Through the ages the cry "en garde!" has reverberated from the walls of gladiator schools, echoed through Spanish oak trees concealing Louisiana dueling grounds, and pierced the clatter of contemporary university fencing classes. The term is functional in the western vocabulary, appearing in popular literature, cartoons, and conversations; yet, it is basically the challenge of the fencer. "En garde!" probably launched the Battle of Crécy (1346), which has been cited as the beginning of modern fencing, although historical records reveal that some form of heavy swordplay was engaged in as daily exercise for military men and upper class citizens in the ancient world and during the Middle Ages.

From the middle of the sixteenth century the popularity of settling disputes by bladework steadily increased throughout Europe, culminating in the great ages of dueling—the sixteenth and seventeenth centuries. As the weapons gradually evolved from cumbersome swords to sabers, and from rapiers to lighter, more flexible foils, the costumes changed from heavy plate armor to cloth. The development in the middle of the seventeenth century of the full mask for face protection initiated the possibilities of fencing as a sport. Those who fenced in the early ages were trained knights and warriors; those who fenced in the eighteenth century were cavaliers, fencing for honor and for enjoyment.

Today fencing is solely a sport. It retains much of the flourish and exhilaration of the battle, but the danger of injury has been eliminated. As a consequence of omitting much of the ritualism and formality, it is a more dynamic and athletic sport. The cavalier was dashing, honorable, and maintained impeccable form. The modern fencer is agile, fast, and intelligent.

# WHAT IS FENCING?

## The Objective

The fencer seeks to touch his opponent without being touched and, ultimately, to win the fencing bout. Theoretically, a defensive maneuver exists for every portion of the target, so that if a fencer were perfect in defense, he could never be touched.

The objective is to beguile the opponent into moving his own blade into the wrong defensive area. Nothing is as satisfying to a fencer as making a clean touch and seeing an expression of surprise flash upon his opponent's face.

A friendly game of fencing is called an assault, but when touches (hits) are counted to determine the winner of an assault it is called a bout. A woman wins a bout by scoring four hits against her opponent before she receives that number, whereas a man wins a bout by first scoring five touches against his opponent. Unless the bout is very informal, a jury of four judges observes the bout and decides upon the validity of the hits. A president of the jury, or director, decides upon issues of right-of-way. In electric foil competition, an electronic scoring device substitutes for the jury, but there is no substitute for the director. As electrical equipment is relatively recent within the history of fencing, non-electric fencing is called conventional fencing or conventional foil, while competition using the electronic scoring device is called electrical fencing.

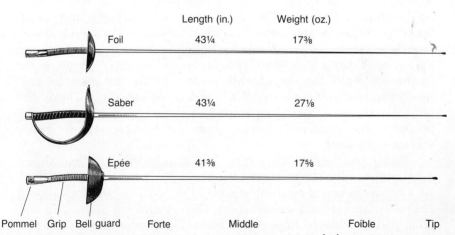

**Figure 1.** Comparisons and nomenclature of foil, épée, and saber.

## The Weapons

Three weapons are currently used in the sport of fencing: the foil, the épée, and the saber. They have many similarities and in several instances are governed by the same rules. However, each has slightly different characteristics, and the style of fencing differs radically in the three weapons. The foil is the basic weapon, and for this reason the scope of this book includes skills, rules, and strategies pertaining only to foil fencing. Techniques and timing learned in foil fencing are easily transferred to épée and saber and, although many men prefer to use the foil only, a great many use the foil to learn the foundations of fencing and then become skilled in one of the other weapons. Some men are proficient with all three weapons and are called "three weapon men."

### The foil

The foil has a light steel rectangular blade with a blunted end or button covered by a rubber tip. It is held by a grip, and the hand is protected by a light piece of steel called a bell guard. The foil blade is quite flexible and bends when the tip comes in contact with an opponent. Thus, a considerable amount of the force of the thrust is absorbed by the springlike bending of the blade rather than by the body. This perhaps is one of the reasons why women fence only with

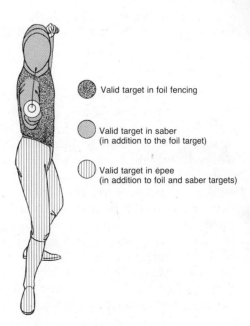

Valid target in foil fencing

Valid target in saber
(in addition to the foil target)

Valid target in épee
(in addition to foil and saber targets)

**Figure 2.** Target area for fencing weapons.

a foil. The electric foil is heavier and stiffer, having an electric body cord that is threaded down the sleeve of the jacket. The cord connects to the bell guard. The tip of an electric foil is called a pointe d'arrêt.

The target in foil fencing is the torso of the fencer. This is smaller than those targets of épée and saber, and it requires much skill and finesse to penetrate an opponent's defense in order to touch. When fencers use electric fencing equipment, they wear a metallic sleeveless vest which covers only valid target area.

Foil fencing is governed by the principle of right-of-way, which means that a fencer is obligated first to defend himself in the event he is attacked, before he may counterattack. Thus, a foil bout is a series of well-executed attacks and parries performed in a sequence. This sequence, or *phrase d'armes*, determines which touch counts in the event that there is not a clear priority in terms of time.

### The épée

The épée is the stiffest and the heaviest of the three weapons. It is a thrusting weapon and is used in bouts composed of five hits or six minutes. The bell guard is very large and the blade is rigid, terminating in a button tip. Because the entire body is target and there are no rules of right-of-way, an épée bout is more like a duel than is a bout with any other weapon. The first man hit is declared touched, regardless of form; if simultaneous touches are made, both men are declared hit. Due to its military history and close resemblance to the rapier that was used in dueling, the épée is the only weapon used in the world Pentathlon competitions.

### The saber

The contemporary saber differs from both the foil and épée in that it is both a cutting and a thrusting weapon. Hits may be scored by a direct thrust to the body or by cutting with the blade. The target in saber fencing reflects the historical use of the saber as a cavalry weapon. Only the torso, head, and arms (i.e., those parts of the body that comprise the exposed target of a man on horseback) are considered valid target area. Five hits or six minutes comprise a saber bout. Because the head is valid target and cutting is also allowed, saber fencing is spectacular and dramatic—a more satisfying spectator sport than a fencing bout using the other two weapons. The steel blade is approximately rectangular near the guard, but tapers to a two-sided narrow strip with a button tip. The guard is a large convex form similar to the foil guard, except that it continues over the knuckles and connects to the grip.

## Field of Play

Although two people may satisfactorily fence informally in their back yard or playroom, the official field of play is the *piste* or terrain, and is spoken of casually by American fencers as "the strip." The strip is usually composed of rubber, plastic, or cork; when electric equipment is used, the *piste* is metallic mesh. It is approximately six feet wide and 39 feet, 4 inches long.

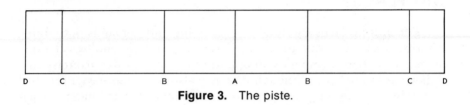

D     C           B       A       B           C     D

**Figure 3.**  The piste.

Seven lines are drawn on the strip parallel to its width.

A. *Center Line.* The exact middle of the strip.

B. *On Guard Line.* The line behind which fencers begin the bout.

C. *Warning Line.* The line that serves to warn the fencer that he is approaching the end of the field of play.

D. *End Line.* Termination of the field of play. If a fencer is driven behind this line twice, he may be penalized by having a touch scored against him.

## Fencing Ethics

The sport of fencing has retained, through the centuries, a code of behavior that reflects the courtly graciousness, eloquence, and gallantry that were the hallmark of the knight or cavalier of the upper class. Equipment is maintained to conform to rigid safety and efficiency standards. The only acceptable fencing uniform is one that is completely white, well tailored, and clean.

The behavior demanded in the fencing rooms or clubs (salle d'armes) and at tournaments is that of modesty, politeness, and self control. Belligerence and braggadocio are not acceptable. Each bout, whether formal or informal, always begins with a formal salute. A simple salute is executed by a fencer when a touch is made against him. It is common to hear a verbal communication such as, "Good move!" in addition to the salute. A formal salute and handshake conclude the bout.

The safety of oneself and one's competitor is of foremost concern to the fencer. No one, no matter how skilled he thinks himself to be, must ever cross blades with another fencer who is not properly protected by mask, jacket, and glove. Even though modern fencing equipment is thoroughly safe when used properly, one must always remember that the weapon can inflict serious injury when used improperly.

## WHY FENCE?

Fencing involves the total human being and demands optimum contributions from the physical, cognitive, and psychological domains. As a sport it provides an opportunity for intensive exercise in a short period of time, although one may also fence more cognitively and rely less on physical resources. Inasmuch as a fencer must constantly analyze defenses and attacks and devise strategies that will enable him to outwit his opponent, fencing demands uncompromising attention to the bout and offers mental challenge of the highest order. Yet, substantial enjoyment may be experienced by the novice using only the most elementary attacks and defenses.

Fencing provides a continuum of complexity and an unlimited range of mental stimulation, as the possible attacks and defenses grow more and more involved and the moment of the final arrival of the touch becomes more and more delayed. Foil work appeals to persons with wide variations in temperament; among the nation's best fencers may be found personalities ranging from the physically aggressive to the cooly deliberate.

Fencing is one of the most convenient leisure sports in which to participate. It requires only two people, it may occur in a rather small area with a low ceiling, and the equipment is portable and quite durable. Because it does not require excessive strength in order to have an enjoyable time and because it is possible to compensate for speed and power with superior strategy, fencing is an exceptionally good coeducational sport. Although men do not compete officially against women, most men and women find fencing with the opposite sex very enjoyable. Indeed, fencing is the only combative sport in which it is socially acceptable for a woman to participate with a man.

Among the attractive characteristics of the sport of fencing is the fact that it is possible to continue participation well into the golden years of life. Rather than being forced to slow down to incompetency as a result of aging, the fencer may find that he becomes more wily and retains his proficiency with increasing years. It is probably one of the very few sports in which one finds competitors on an international level who are over the age of 50.

## Recreational Fencing

The sport of fencing is attracting more and more participants each year. A probable reason is the growing number of opportunities for people to receive instruction at a nominal cost. Until the latter part of the twentieth century, only those who could afford to take private lessons from a fencing master became proficient at the sport. Today fencing teachers are introducing beginning fencing skills in YMCAs and YWCAs, recreation centers, university and high school physical education departments, theatrical schools, and modeling and finishing schools. Fencing clubs (salles) have been established in almost every major city in the United States. Most of these clubs have a qualified fencing master who gives private lessons at reduced rates to all members of the club and to others at reasonable cost. The club activity is generally casual fencing, with occasional tournaments or parties. Some clubs have "couple contests," in which the best male fencer and the weakest woman fencer compete as a pair. The woman begins the bout against another woman, and they fence until one of them has received four touches. Their male partners continue the bout, but each begins with his partner's score. The bout is completed when one of the pairs has had ten touches scored against them.

The camaraderie existing among fencers, and developed through club membership, transcends language, philosophical, and political barriers. It provides common experiences and knowledge among people from all vocations and professions.

## Competitive Fencing

Serious fencing students will be "compelled" to compete. The excitement, glamour, and mystique of the ancient duel are very closely approximated in the competitive situation, and the ultimate test of the fencer's cunning and ability is his final rank in a fencing competition. Becoming a high level competitor requires diligence, determination, and many hours of lessons and training. The tournament competitor has knowledge and abilities far beyond those presented in this book. Additionally, almost all tournaments utilize electric scoring equipment, so that the serious student must learn to fence in a somewhat different style dictated by the electric equipment. A discussion of fencing with electric equipment is presented later in the book.

Competitive fencing in the United States is governed by the Amateur Fencers League of America (AFLA). This association generally follows the rules enacted by the Federation Internationale d'Escrime (FIE), which governs international competitions. Regional and local divisions of the AFLA sponsor many tournaments for each of several classifications throughout the year. A competitor is classified as Prep, Novice, Junior, or Open, depending upon his skill. Points are awarded on the basis of performance in tournaments and the level of the tournament. Successful competitors on the local level qualify to participate in the annual national tournament. National winners usually qualify for the United States Olympic Fencing Team or other touring teams.

Many college students represent their schools in intercollegiate conference competition. Additionally, competitions for men are conducted by the National Collegiate Athletic Association, and for women by the Division for Girls and Women's Sports of the American Association for Health, Physical Education, and Recreation.

## Theatrical Fencing

For the student of the theater, fencing is an interesting recreational activity that may also be utilized in period acting. Many Shakespearean plays contain scenes in which duels are a component. Theatrical fencing is a highly complex form of fencing that must be choreographed and learned. The illusion of danger and the heat of battle must be provided while, at the same time, the safety of the actors must be maintained. Theatrical fencing requires knowledge of combat with the sword and shield, net and trident, two-handed sword, rapier and cloak, and rapier and dagger.

## CHAPTER 2

# EQUIPMENT

## EQUIPMENT AND ITS CARE

All that is needed in the way of equipment for the beginning fencer is a jacket, mask, foil, and glove. Many schools and fencing clubs supply half-jackets or practice jackets, foils, masks, and gloves to beginning fencers. If you plan to fence recreationally or competitively, however, you will want to purchase your own equipment. If possible, it is helpful to buy two of each piece of equipment, so that when you have an unexpected guest who enjoys fencing you will have the needed equipment. Several fencing companies, as well as sporting goods stores, carry foils, masks and gloves. It is wise to buy fencing clothing custom-made from the fencing companies, because the movements that you will need to make can only be accomplished when you are wearing properly fitted and appropriate clothing.

## Fencing Jacket

The jacket should be a white regulation jacket that is long sleeved, with a groin strap passing between the legs and buckling to the back. This strap holds the lower front of the jacket in place. It is highly desirable that the jacket be large enough to allow the fencer mobility; on the other hand, it must be snug so that there is no excess fold or bit of material that will provide additional and unwanted target. Most fencing companies supply a diagram on which you may supply your own torso measurements and thus purchase a custom-made, good fitting jacket.

Women's jackets have two inside cotton pockets that are designed to stabilize breast protectors in position during a bout. Breast protectors are not necessary when fencing with conventional foil, but they are mandatory when fencing with the more rigid electric foil. Protectors may be purchased from fencing companies. These protec-

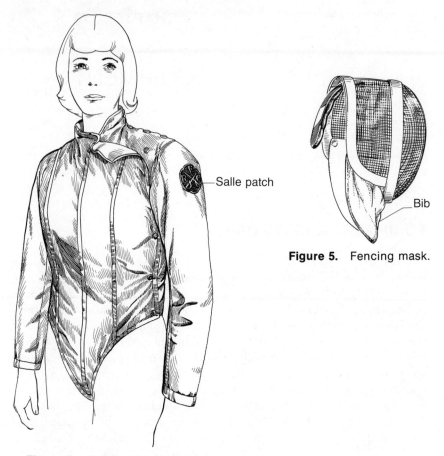

—Salle patch

—Bib

**Figure 5.**  Fencing mask.

**Figure 4.**  Full fencing jacket.

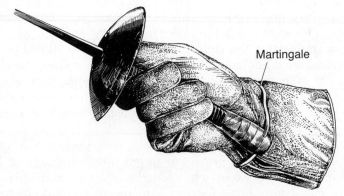

Martingale

**Figure 6.**  Glove and martingale.

tors are generally round, aluminum, cone shaped disks. Some women construct their own out of leather, and some just use a double thickness of small aluminum pie pans.

If you are enrolled in a class in which a fencing jacket is provided, you may discover that the jacket has only one sleeve. These jackets are practice jackets and are quite acceptable for beginning fencers. They also have the advantage in the warmer climates of being a somewhat cooler jacket in which to practice. They are not, however, acceptable in fencing tournaments. The jacket shown in Figure 4 is a full jacket and has a salle patch sewn on the left sleeve. The salle patch indicates the fencing club or salle for which the fencer competes.

A jacket should be washed after each fencing session. Inasmuch as it is long sleeved, it absorbs much perspiration during a workout. Accumulations of perspiration will stain the jacket and weaken the fiber, causing it to wear out sooner. A clean jacket is more flexible and thus more comfortable.

## The Mask

The mask is wire mesh and leather with an insertable cloth bib that protects the neck. If you purchase a mask, it would be wise to purchase an insulated one in the event that you later choose to fence with electric equipment. Insulated masks have transparent plastic coating the wire mesh. Be sure that the mask has a bib that can be snapped in and out, so that it may be washed each time the jacket is washed.

## The Glove

The glove is usually a soft kid practice glove, which has several thicknesses of padding on the back side. Be certain that the glove fits; a skimpy one inhibits finger dexterity, and a bulky one makes it difficult to retain the foil grip during a fencing phrase.

## The Martingale

A martingale is a leather strap that holds the foil grip firmly next to the wrist. Many French foils have a hole in the pommel, through which the martingale is threaded. In this case, the martingale may be a thin leather strap that looks much like a shoe string. With Italian or pistol grip foils, some fencers just use a wide leather strap that buckles. In either case, the purpose of the martingale is to prevent the foil from being struck from your hand so that it flies across the room or crashes into spectators. The martingale is a safety device, and is not intended to substitute for the proper positioning and gripping of your foil hand (see Fig. 6). When an electric foil is used, the body cord, which is threaded through your sleeve and attached to the bell guard, also serves the safety purpose of the martingale; therefore, a martingale is not required by the rules of electric fencing. Many fencers, particularly those of the French school, prefer to omit the martingale when possible. They feel that it binds the grip to their arm so tightly that it robs them of a certain amount of finesse. Those of the Italian school employ a more forceful approach, and therefore enjoy the additional security that a firmly secured martingale provides.

## The Foil

The foil blade and bell guard must be regulation in terms of length, weight, flexibility, and construction. The grip, however, may be any of several styles. Some fencers prefer the straight lines of the French foil, while others prefer the additional support of the Italian or American "pistol" grip. A few fencers buy plastic pistol type grips and literally carve a grip with a knife to fit the shape of their hand.

The blade should be cared for by occasionally sanding with steel wool and oiling to prevent rust. It should be stored in a dry place, and hung by the grip or bell guard when not in use. The foil should

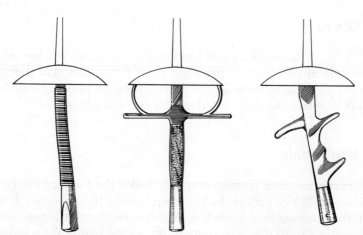

**Figure 7.**   Three styles of foil grip; from left to right: French, Italian and pistol grip.

never be thrown or stored on the floor. Occasionally it is necessary to replace the bell guard pad; sometimes it is necessary to replace the blade. Extra blades should be purchased with the foil, and they are easily replaced when broken. Never use any type of substitute for a foil blade, and never fence with a broken one, even if only a tiny part of it is missing. A broken blade is extremely sharp and dangerous.

## Equipment Bag

A canvas bag with a handle is available for easy transporting and storage of fencing equipment. It is well worth the money, as it is designed to hold the odd shapes of several masks, foils, gloves, and other paraphernalia of the fencer. Fencers who compete usually carry their own tools for quick adjustment or repair of their clothing or equipment, and the extra pockets that are supplied on the carrying bag are convenient to carry such things as adhesive tape, pocket-knives, pliers, screw drivers, and rubber fencing tips, not to mention pocket money, comb, and handkerchief.

## Clothing

Most fencers wear a very light cotton T-shirt under the fencing jacket. Covering the full length of the legs is mandatory for competition and is preferred for recreational fencing. Most fencers purchase knee length trousers that buckle or fasten with Velcro just below the knee. White knee length socks are tucked up under the knee buckle, and white tennis shoes or special leather-soled fencing shoes are worn.

Although the majority of competitors wear knee length fencing trousers, a few wear full length trousers that fasten at the ankle. Both men's and women's fencing trousers zip or button at the side, since buttons in the front of the trousers would cause additional folds of material which are undesirable in a valid target area.

## Hair

Long hair must not hang over any part of the target, as it is difficult for judges of conventional foil to judge the validity of a touch if it occurs amongst strands of hair. Additionally, hair serves as insulation between the electric foil button tip and the copper vest and prevents touches from registering on an electric recording device. Long hair should be caught back and fastened behind the neck.

## CHAPTER 3

# CONDITIONING

Fencing is a much more vigorous sport than most people realize. It requires energy expenditure in the most demanding form possible—through power movements. Since many movements, in order to be successful, must reach full velocity as rapidly as possible after being initiated from a motionless position, great demands are placed on the neuromuscular system of the body. The fencer must be not only strong and enduring but flexible and capable of absorbing the strain of changing directions suddenly.

The ultimate performance in fencing involves complete mental attention devoted to an opponent who is constantly changing his distance from you, his aggressiveness in terms of attacking or defending, and his foil-arm positions. The fencer must be continually analyzing the opponent's strategies while creating and modifying his own strategies; he therefore should not be forced—in addition to this—to consider whether he has enough strength to perform an attack or whether he has enough endurance to attack several times in succession. Naturally, the more easily the body responds to the demands of the competitor, the less he has to be concerned with them. A fencer who is agonizing over breath and aching legs has his attention diverted and sacrifices some wiliness and cunning that he may have been able to bring to the task earlier in the bout. For these reasons, conditioning exercises are essential to the fencer who chooses to make fencing the exhilarating, intellectual, and challenging sport that it can be.

Conditioning is specific to the activity. Specific, as used in this sense, means that you develop only what you train. Research has shown that no one type of training or participation in one sport will prepare you for all types of activity. If you wish strength in certain muscle groups, you must exercise those muscle groups, not others. If you wish endurance in specific muscles, you must exercise those particular muscle groups under a light load for a longer period of time. Relatively little carry over in terms of strength and endurance exists from one sport to another, or from one activity to another. Specificity of training permeates all phases of conditioning. When you hear a friend say, "I can't understand it, I thought I was in shape! I swim almost every day, but after playing two hours of tennis yesterday I am so sore I can hardly move," you are hearing him express the principle of specificity of training.

A conditioning program is designed to develop your body so that you can achieve specific goals. Your goal may be simply to develop an overall moderate efficiency in the functioning of your heart, lungs, joints, and muscle. In other words, you may aspire to a moderate level of physical fitness with which you can complete your tasks of a normal day without undue fatigue. Additionally, a moderate level of fitness will enable you to meet minor emergencies of physical demand without accruing physical injury. This level of physical fitness provides a reserve of strength that enables you to walk through life with a spring in your step and a substantial resiliency and resistance to stress. This general level of physical fitness satisfies many persons' needs. The activity of fencing, if you participate two or three times weekly, will certainly contribute toward your achievement of this goal.

Your goal may be, however, to attain a higher level of physiological and psychological functioning than that required for minimal physical fitness levels. If you wish to be an above average fencer, or to achieve the optimum benefits from the activity of fencing, then you will want to develop superb neuromuscular functioning and endurance in the specific set of neuromuscular patterns that make up the physical skills of fencing.

Whatever your goal is, the requisites of a successful conditioning program are consistency, dedication, and the use of the correct techniques. Consistency of training is essential to an increase in physical condition. You must train every day and unwaveringly follow the schedule that you establish for yourself. If you are scheduled to execute 10 sit-ups each day for one week, it will not do for you to skip three days and then do 40 sit-ups on the fourth day. Dedication to your training schedule implies the seriousness of purpose which you bring to the conditioning exercises and the enthusiasm with which you complete them. If your schedule calls for an all-out run for one minute, then it must be an all-out run, not a half-hearted jog. Your consistency and dedication represent your attitudinal approach to the training schedule. Your attitude reflects your commitment to your goals. Regardless of the level of physical functioning you aspire to attain, you must be consistent and dedicated.

Not everyone wants to be a champion fencer. As a matter of fact, few do. But if you are one of these few, then you must follow a rigorous training schedule. Many of the coaches of this country have declared that the basic inadequacy of our American fencers in international competitions has been that of inferior training, not inferior skill or technique.

A successful conditioning program is also based upon sound principle and utilizes correct techniques. Basically, a good conditioning program is designed to develop (a) strength, (b) muscular endurance, (c) cardiovascular respiratory endurance, (d) flexibility, and (e) power. Several exercises to develop each of these components of conditioning are presented in this chapter. Suggestions in terms of duration and intensity of exercise are made for those who plan a rigorous training schedule in preparation for serious fencing competition. If this is not your goal, simply reduce the repetitions, duration, or intensity suggested for each exercise. You may also reduce the effect of a conditioning program by lengthening the period of time between the exercises that you do. A conditioning program chart is provided on pages 24 and 25 so that you may record your progress.

## DEVELOPING STRENGTH

To make a muscle stronger you must overload it. The principle of overload—a well established physiological phenomenon—means that in order to develop strength you must make the muscles work with slightly more load on them than they can manipulate comfortably. The muscles should work under a strain, perhaps even under a load that they cannot budge, for a short period of time. This type of work is characteristically slow and sustained, and should be included in every workout of the conditioning program.

Two methods of overloading muscle are isometric exercises and isotonic exercises against resistance. You have probably heard of isometric exercises, for the concept of isometric exercise has been widely publicized. Briefly, isometric exercise is contraction of the muscle against a force that is so great that the muscle does not change its length, or shorten. When you push your right hand against your left hand as hard as you can so that neither hand moves, you have performed an isometric exercise. Isotonic exercise occurs when a muscle contracts to a different length. To increase strength, isotonic exercise must occur with resistance, such as when you move your limb while holding a weight through a range of motion of your joint. For example, when you complete a deep knee bend you have isotonically exercised. Your thigh and leg muscles have moved, while supporting the weight of your body through the range of motion of your hip, knee, and ankle joints. If you lift a heavy weight such as a dumbbell through a range of motion, you are also isotonically exercising. If you stop the dumbbell half way through the range of motion and hold it motionless, you are isometrically exercising.

The following exercises for developing strength use both isometric and isotonic contraction. Because most people do not have weights or other apparatus with which to overload muscle, many of the exercises listed in this book use gravity as resistance. Another technique for providing resistance is the use of a partner to hold one of your body segments so that it will not move. In any event, all of the exercises for strength development are constructed so that they will overload the muscle groups.

Each exercise is described as a unit called a set. For example, if the exercise calls for 5 right leg lifts followed by 5 left leg lifts, then to repeat 4 sets of this exercise you would have to repeat the exercise, as written, 3 more times (a total of 20 right leg lifts and 20 left leg lifts).

**Figure 8.**   Lower leg extension exercise.

1. *Lower Leg Extension.* Sit on a table with your hands in your lap. Have a partner hold his hand against the top of your ankle. Try to raise your right lower leg to a horizontal position while your partner provides just enough resistance against the lift so that you have to work to lift it. Relax your right leg, and then try to raise your left leg against your partner's hand.

2. *Lower Leg Flexion.* Lie on your stomach with your feet and lower legs at right angles to your thighs. Your partner holds your ankles and resists your efforts to bring your heels to your hips.

3. *Leg Extension.* Lie on your back with your feet flat against a wall and your knees bent. Attempt to straighten out your legs so that

**Figure 9.**    Lower leg flexion exercise.

**Figure 10.**    Leg extension exercise.

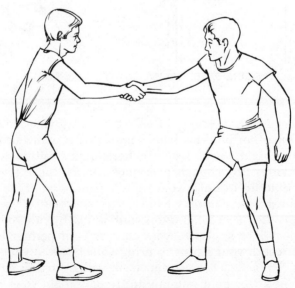

**Figure 11.**    Wrist rotation exercise.

you slide backward on the floor. Have your partner push against your shoulders so that you have to extend your legs with effort in order to straighten them out.

4. *Hand Gripping.* Grip a small handball or tennis ball as hard as you can. Hold the gripping action for 10 seconds.

5. *Wrist Rotation.* Clasp hands in a handshake position with your partner. While in this position, each of you attempts a counter-clockwise rotation. Hold the attempt for 10 seconds.

## DEVELOPING MUSCULAR ENDURANCE

The principle that endurance is specific to the task dictates that you do exercises each day that involve the movements and positions that are used in fencing. Muscular endurance is not the same as cardiovascular endurance. The former is the ability of the particular muscle to continue contraction over a period of time; the latter refers to the ability of the body cells to obtain and use oxygen and to rid the body of carbon dioxide.

In order to develop muscular endurance for fencing, you must perform exercises against resistance that are as similar to the movements of fencing as possible. Fencing footwork, in the on guard position, should be practiced over and over each day until the legs are conditioned to maintain body weight for long periods of time in the on guard position. See the descriptions of the fencing techniques listed below in Chapter 4.

1. *Lunge.* Lunge 10 times (one set) daily the first week.

2. *Advance-Retreat.* Advance 10 times, followed by 10 retreats. Progressively increase the number of advance-retreat sets according to the conditioning program chart directions.

3. *Advance-Lunge.* Advance-lunge 10 times successively. Progressively increase the number of advance-lunge sets.

4. *Thrusts.* Stand in the on guard position close enough to a wall so that you can hit it by a full thrust without a lunge. Thrust rapidly and successively 10 times.

5. *Sprinter-Starts.* Place both hands on the floor in front of you, your right knee bent and your right foot slightly behind your hands, and your left leg stretched out behind you. Alternate leg positions rapidly 10 times.

6. *Russian Bear Dance.* Start in a squat position with your arms folded across your chest. Extend your right leg out fully forward and diagonal to your body, while you fling your arms outward. Return to the squat position. Follow by extending your left leg out full and your arms out. Continue alternating right and left leg extensions until each leg has been extended 5 times.

**Figure 12.**  Sprinter starts.

## DEVELOPING CARDIOVASCULAR-RESPIRATORY ENDURANCE

A high level of cardiovascular-respiratory endurance is desirable and may be developed by running, riding a bicycle, or jumping a rope. To follow the progression chart suggestions for development of cardiovascular-respiratory endurance, choose one of the three exercises listed below and complete it at least four times a week.

1. *Running.* Run one-quarter mile. You may need to begin this exercise by running as long as possible and walking when you are tired.

Position 1                          Position 2
**Figure 13.**  Russian bear dance.

2. *Bicycling.* Ride a bicycle for one mile.

3. *Rope Jumping.* Jump rope for one minute without stopping.

## DEVELOPING FLEXIBILITY

The fourth component of this conditioning program is the development of flexibility. Flexibility is necessary for any sport that requires agility for top performance. Agility is the ability to move the body in successively quick changes of direction, both forward and backward and up and down. This is, of course, the foundation of fencing and is termed fencing mobility. The championship calibre fencers are extremely mobile, and the modern fencing bout is a performance of extreme agility and quickness. The body must be flexible to sustain the sudden lurches and dramatic changes of direction. Ankle, knee, hip, and back flexibility are all desirable. For this reason, stretching movements on both sides of the body are in order.

1. *Toe Touch.* Stand with your legs together and attempt to touch your toes without bending your knees. Try to touch your toes 5 times.

2. *Lunge Stretch.* Assume a deep lunge position and bounce gently over your front knee. Bounce 5 times. Slowly try to extend your back leg more and more behind you on each bounce. Shift into a lunge position on the other leg and bounce 5 times.

3. *Lunge and Arm-Stretch.* Assume the lunge position described in 2. Slowly stretch your arms over your head as you bounce 5 times over the right knee. Repeat over the left knee.

4. *Arm Circles.* Swing your arms in vertical circles 5 times forward and five times backward.

5. *Arm Flings.* Stand with feet astride and arms horizontally folded across the chest. Fling the arms backward and behind the

**Figure 14.** Lunge-stretch.

| STRENGTH EXERCISES Week | Number of Sets Recommended | | | | | | | | | | | |
|---|---|---|---|---|---|---|---|---|---|---|---|---|
| | 1 | 2 | 3 | 4 | 5 | 6 | 7 | 8 | 9 | 10 | 11 | 12 |
| 1. Lower Leg Extension | 2 | 2 | 3 | 3 | 4 | 4 | 3 | 3 | 3 | 3 | 3 | 3 |
| 2. Lower Leg Flexion | 2 | 2 | 3 | 3 | 4 | 4 | 3 | 3 | 3 | 3 | 3 | 3 |
| 3. Leg Extension | 3 | 3 | 4 | 4 | 5 | 5 | 5 | 5 | 5 | 6 | 6 | 6 |
| 4. Hand Gripping | 4 | 4 | 4 | 4 | 5 | 5 | 5 | 5 | 4 | 4 | 4 | 4 |
| 5. Wrist Rotation | 2 | 2 | 2 | 2 | 2 | 2 | 2 | 2 | 2 | 2 | 2 | 2 |
| MUSCULAR ENDURANCE | | | | | | | | | | | | |
| 1. Lunge | 2 | 3 | 4 | 5 | 6 | 6 | 6 | 7 | 7 | 8 | 8 | 8 |
| 2. Advance-Retreat | 2 | 2 | 3 | 3 | 4 | 4 | 4 | 4 | 5 | 5 | 6 | 6 |
| 3. Advance-Lunge | 2 | 2 | 3 | 4 | 4 | 4 | 5 | 5 | 5 | 6 | 6 | 6 |
| 4. Thrusts | 1 | 2 | 2 | 2 | 3 | 3 | 3 | 3 | 4 | 4 | 3 | 3 |
| 5. Sprinter Starts | 1 | 1 | 2 | 2 | 2 | 2 | 2 | 2 | 2 | 2 | 3 | 3 |
| 6. Russian Bear Dance | 1 | 1 | 1 | 1 | 1 | 1 | 2 | 2 | 2 | 2 | 2 | 2 |

**Figure 16.** Conditioning Program Chart: Suggestions for progression of exercises to develop strength, muscular endurance, cardiovascular endurance, flexibility, and power. When you complete the recommended exercise, check the block it is in so that you will remember from day to day what you have done.

| CARDIOVASCULAR RESPIRATORY ENDURANCE | Week | 1 | 2 | 3 | 4 | 5 | 6 | 7 | 8 | 9 | 10 | 11 | 12 |
|---|---|---|---|---|---|---|---|---|---|---|---|---|---|
| | | | | | | Number of Sets Recommended | | | | | | | |
| 1. Running<br>2. Bicycle Riding<br>3. Rope Jumping | | 1 | 2 | 4 | 4 | 4 | 6 | 6 | 8 | 8 | 8 | 8 | 8 |
| FLEXIBILITY EXERCISES | | | | | | | | | | | | | |
| 1. Toe Touch<br>2. Lunge Stretch<br>3. Lunge and Arm Stretch<br>4. Arm Circles<br>5. Arm Flings<br>6. Sitting Stretch | | 1 | 1 | 1 | 1 | 1 | 1 | 1 | 1 | 1 | 1 | 1 | 1 |
| POWER EXERCISES | | | | | | | | | | | | | |
| 1. Speed Lunges | | 1 | 1 | 1 | 1 | 1 | 1 | 2 | 2 | 2 | 2 | 2 | 2 |
| 2. Jumping | | 1 | 1 | 2 | 2 | 2 | 2 | 3 | 3 | 3 | 3 | 4 | 4 |
| 3. Forward Jumps | | 1 | 1 | 1 | 1 | 1 | 1 | 2 | 2 | 2 | 2 | 2 | 2 |
| 4. Running in Place | | 1 | 1 | 1 | 1 | 2 | 2 | 2 | 2 | 3 | 3 | 4 | 4 |

**Figure 16.**  *Continued.*

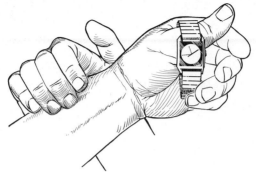

**Figure 17.** Taking your pulse rate. Wrist watch with second hand is used.

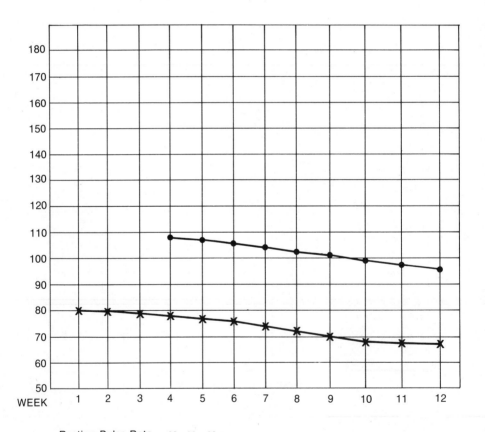

Resting Pulse Rate    ✕—✕—✕

Recovery Pulse Rate    ●—●—●    (Recorded exactly 2 minutes following a one mile [4 sets] run)

**Figure 18.** See opposite page for legend.

To time the recovery pulse rate, run the mile. As you cross the finish line, start looking at your watch and time exactly two minutes. The instant the two minutes is completed, begin a 15 second count of your pulse. Multiply that figure by 4 and this is your recovery pulse rate. As you improve in your physical condition, you will note that it takes less and less time for your pulse rate to return near to the resting level.

**Figure 18.** Pulse Rate Change Chart: the record is a hypothetical one. Record your own pulse rate on the graph. Both resting and recovery pulse rates are very different for each person, so do not expect yours to look exactly like this hypothetical one.

## CHAPTER 4

# BASIC SKILLS

Fencing is somewhat analogous to chess; the moves of each piece must be learned before the player is free to concentrate on outwitting his opponent. Fencing, of course, involves the attainment of physical skill as well as knowledge of strategy. The beginning skills of foil fencing are basic to potential success and ultimate enjoyment. Some of the initial skills that you will practice — such as footwork, the fencing position, and some simple defenses — are not in themselves like fencing a bout. You must be patient in the first few weeks of fencing instruction and try to perfect the foundation skills; for the more perfectly you can execute these skills, the more you can implement your strategies. Inasmuch as the majority of fencers are right-handed, the directions in this book are written from the right-handed fencer's point of view. A left-hander need only reverse the directions.

## THE GRIP

These directions for gripping the foil are written for the French foil, which is generally used by beginning fencers. Other styles of

**Table 1.** Common Errors in Gripping the Foil

| Error | Cause | Correction |
|---|---|---|
| 1. Foil upside down. | 1A. Inattention. | 1A. Place thumb on top of grip. |
| 2. Fatigued hand. | 2A. Holding grip too tightly. | 2A. Spread last three fingers slightly. |
| | | 2B. Let little finger rest off the grip if this feels more natural. |
| 3. Foil not an extension of arm. | 3A. Pommel hanging below the wrist. | 3A. Grip the foil in a relaxed manner; try to feel the grip of the foil nestling in the groove between your thumb and little finger muscles. |
| | 3B. Pommel above wrist. | 3B. Relax the wrist, being certain that wrist and forearm make a straight line. |

foil handle are gripped similarly. Hold the foil at the forte in the palm of your left hand, so that the blade bends upward and points away from your body. With the right hand, place (a) your thumb flatly on top of the grip ¼ inch away from the inside of the bell guard, (b) the back of your index finger underneath the grip and against the felt pad lining the guard, (c) the pommel in the middle of the inside of your wrist, and the last three fingers naturally on the inside of the grip.

## Drills for the Grip

1. Take the grip several times with your eyes shut.
2. Pick the foil up from the floor with your right hand and manipulate it with that hand only until you have the proper grip.
3. Have a partner hold the foil at arm's length, varying from a correct to incorrect grip position. See if you can detect when the grip is correct.
4. Have a partner place several right- and left-handed foils together on the floor. Sort them into right- and left-handed foils.

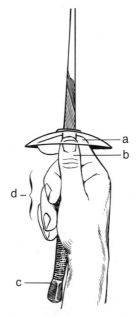

**Figure 19.** The French foil grip: (a) index finger next to bell guard pad, (b) thumb flat on top of grip, (c) pommel next to wrist, and (d) fingers flat on medial side of grip.

## Practice Hints

1. Be sure that your foil and forearm appear to be one unbroken line.

2. Keep your pommel pressed firmly against your wrist at all times during practice. If your hand becomes too fatigued to maintain the correct pommel position, stop practicing for a while.

3. Make all blade movements as small as possible by completing them with only minimal contractions and relaxations of the last three fingers of the grip.

4. Guide the blade with your thumb and index finger.


## ATTENTION AND SALUTE

The position of attention is taken at the beginning of the bout, while you are saluting the opponent, and after each touch has been made in the bout. To assume the position of attention, place your (a) right toe pointing toward your opponent, with your heels together and feet at right angles, (b) right shoulder pointing toward your opponent, and (c) foil arm straight, pointing diagonally downward so that the foil tip is approximately 3 inches from the floor. Tuck your mask away in the curve of your left arm.

The salute may be simple or formal. The simple salute is accomplished by raising the foil from the low diagonal in the position of attention to a position that is vertical. The bell guard should be close to the nose, and the back of the right hand facing the opponent. The blade is then whipped quickly to the low diagonal position. The formal salute, at the beginning and end of the bout, is used to acknowledge the judges, director, and opponent. It is said that the form of the salute comes from the habit of the early duelers, who had a crucifix attached to their bell guard and prior to a duel would kiss the crucifix in order to bring a greater power to their aid. To execute a formal salute:

1. Raise the foil from the low diagonal position of attention to a horizontal position pointing to the right of the body.

2. Bring the foil to a vertical position, bell guard close to your nose, foil tip pointing to the ceiling.

3. Point the foil diagonally and horizontally to the left of your body.

4. Return the foil to position described in number 2.

5. Point the foil straight ahead toward your opponent.

6. Return the foil to number 2 position.

7. Whip the foil back to the low diagonal position.

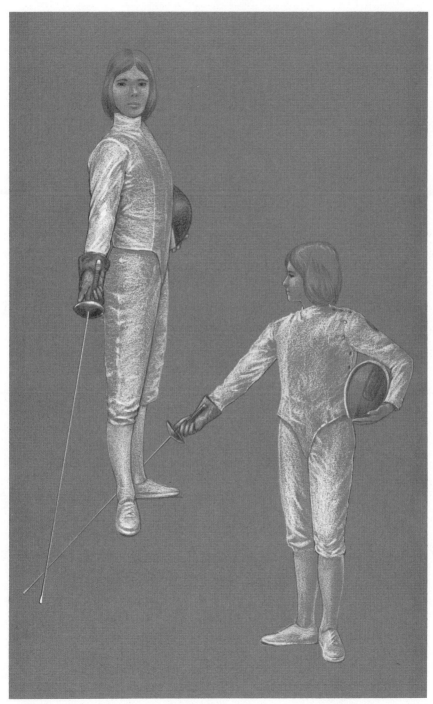

**Figure 20.** Position of attention: right toe straight ahead, right shoulder facing opponent, foil tip 3″ above floor, and mask tucked under left arm.

**Figure 21.** Simple salute.

## Drills for Position of Attention and Salutes

1. Look in a mirror while assuming the position of attention. See if you can present such a profile that only your right shoulder and right leg can be seen.

2. Check, in a mirror, your lower back. If you are "swaybacked," tuck your hips under.

# ON GUARD POSITION

The on guard position is the basic position of readiness from which the fencer makes attacks and defenses. You should feel perfectly balanced in this position. Strong legs and hips are necessary to maintain the position for long periods of time. If you have had any exposure to karate, judo, or ballet you will find that the flexibility and strength developed in these activities enables you to settle comfortably into the fencing on guard position and to learn footwork patterns very quickly.

Although the on guard position described below is mechanically the most efficient, you may find a slight modification necessary to adapt the position to your particular body shape. To assume the on guard position, take the position of attention, then place your right foot forward about two lengths of your shoe. Shift your weight so that it is directly over an imaginary spot exactly between your feet. Keeping your torso straight and your hips tucked under, "sit" down until your knees are above the top of each foot. Bring your foil from the low diagonal position to one in which the tip is pointing at your opponent's neck (your foil elbow should be bent, approximately 6 inches away from your body). The foil hand should be positioned so that the palm is up (Fig. 23). Consider the foil to be an extension of your arm, so that you have an unbroken line from your elbow to the tip of the foil.

To position your left (non-foil) arm, (a) bring your straight arm to a horizontal position that is parallel with the floor, (b) bend your elbow, keeping your upper arm horizontal so that your forearm is vertical and forms a right angle with your upper arm, and (c) relax your wrist so that your hand and fingers are completely limp and hanging toward the floor.

Remember to keep your left arm pulled back away from your chest, for as you pull your left arm back it tends to expose only a profile of your target to your opponent. Note the position of the left arm in Figure 25a. It is pulled back so far that it can barely be seen by the opponent. This arm position has rotated the torso so that very

**Figure 22.**   On guard position: side view.

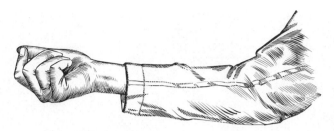

**Figure 23.** Foil hand in on guard position: foil omitted for unobstructed view of the hand position.

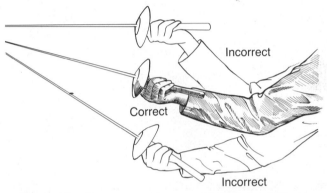

**Figure 24.** Correct and incorrect foil-arm positions.

little target is visible. Conversely, in Figure 25*b* the left arm is allowed to shift forward, thus rotating the entire torso toward the opponent. You can see that there is more observable target to attack in Figure 25*b* than there is in 25*a*. In addition, when the left arm is allowed to remain in a forward position, it is tempting for the beginning fencer to draw the left arm across the target in an attempt to protect the torso. This reflex movement, once initiated, is extremely difficult to inhibit. Some beginners have even developed the habit of attempting to grasp an approaching foil with the left hand. This is, of course, absolutely forbidden by the rules and is penalized—after a warning—by the director's award of a touch against the offender. The best practice is to pay close attention from the very beginning to the correct left arm position.

**Figure 25.** Incorrect (*b*) and correct (*a*) nonfoil-arm positions.

**Table 2.** Common Errors in Assuming the On Guard Position

| Error | Cause | Correction |
| --- | --- | --- |
| 1. Poor balance. | 1A. Feet too close together or too far apart. | 1A. Measure two shoe lengths between feet, and place feet in new position. |
| | 1B. Knees rotated inward. | 1B. Turn left toe slightly outward; use some stretching exercises to provide a wider range of motion at the hip joints. |
| 2. Too much target exposed to opponent. | 2A. Left (non-foil) arm is flexed too far forward, pulling the torso out of profile. | 2A. Concentrate on keeping left arm pulled back. |
| | | 2B. Use stretching exercises to provide more flexibility in shoulders. |
| | | 2C. Practice assuming the on guard position in front of a mirror; try to present as lean a profile as possible. |
| 3. Pain in legs while in on guard position. | 3A. Lack of conditioning. | 3A. See Chapter 3. |
| | 3B. Weight unevenly distributed. | 3B. Practice balancing the weight over an imaginary spot between your feet. |

## Drills for the On Guard Position

1. Lift your front foot and "tap" it 5 or 6 times. If your weight is too much on your front foot, you will be unable to lift your front toe.

2. Alternate 5 times in succession from the position of attention to the on guard position.

3. Look in a full length mirror while facing it. You should see (a) only your right side and leg, (b) your point at neck level, and (c) only half of your left foot.

4. Compare your reflection in drill 3 above with Figure 25a.

5. Stand in front of a mirror in such a position that it will reflect a side view of your on guard position. Compare your position to that in Figure 22.

## Practice Hints

1. Practice until you are able to get into the on guard position without looking at your feet.

2. Continually remind yourself to keep your left arm pulled back behind you so that you present only a profile to your opponent.

## FOOTWORK

Mobility is the earmark of modern fencing. Today's fencing bouts are characterized by stealthy, cautious movement where a play of the blades, feinting, and preparatory arm movements are made suddenly to be interrupted by explosive body action, a flurry of blades, and fantastic speed. You must achieve great agility, much of which can be gained by acquiring proper footwork.

Basic patterns of body mobility that enable the fencer to move forward and backward, as well as to close the distance to the opponent, are the advance, retreat, lunge, and advance-lunge. These footwork patterns enable you to make up lost distance rapidly, retreat out of attack range quickly, and change from attack to defense instantly. The on guard position and the footwork patterns are designed to provide stability as well.

### Advance

Lift your front foot and place it forward a distance that is about the length of your foot. Your heel should contact the floor first. Bring

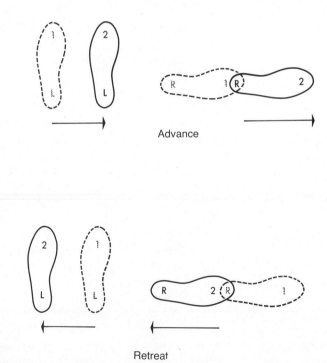

**Figure 26.** Foot patterns of the advance and retreat; dotted lines are first position and solid lines are position following the advance or retreat.

your rear foot forward about the same distance that you moved your front foot (Fig. 26). You should now be in the same on guard position, with the weight evenly distributed over the center of your base of support, except that you have advanced forward slightly. The advance should be done crisply and rather quickly.

### Retreat

Step backward with the rear foot about the distance of half of your foot length; then bring the front foot backward the same distance. The shifts of weight during the advance and retreat should be made as subtly as possible, and the center of body weight should always be over an imaginary spot between the feet. The feet should not be lifted more than an inch or two from the floor during movement, nor should any one foot stay off the floor any longer than necessary.

### Lunge and recovery

The lunge is the footwork foundation of an attack, and the fastest way for you to close the distance between you and your opponent. Generally, the movement sequence of the lunge is a thrust of the foil arm into a straight position, followed by a powerful extension of the back leg. This sequence is critical to a successful attack; it is not just "good form." The rules of fencing demand that you initiate "right-of-way" before you execute a lunge, and the quickest, most effective method of establishing right-of-way is to straighten your foil arm. The forward motion of the foil so that the foil point is menacing your opponent's target is, actually, the definition of right-of-way. An attack, therefore, that is not preceded by this initial foil-arm extension, may be unrecognized by the director. A touch you make as the result of an attack without right-of-way may not be allowed. For this reason, it is wise to develop a lunge that is automatically preceded by a foil-arm thrust.

The specific technique of the lunge is as follows: from the on guard position extend the foil arm so that the foil tip is aiming at your opponent's upper chest. Your palm should be up and your elbow should be as straight as possible without being locked. A locked elbow takes a bit more time to unlock, and inasmuch as quick movements of the arm are essential, it is best to avoid the locked elbow.

As you feel your foil arm reaching full extension, lift your front foot, toe first, and fully extend your back leg. Your body weight shifts forward to a position slightly behind the front foot. All the power and thrust of the lunge is supplied by the back leg and thigh extensor

**Figure 27.** Advance and retreat: side view. (Drawn from Castello, H., and Castello, J.: Fencing. © 1960, The Ronald Press Company, New York.)

**Figure 28.**   Foil-arm thrust: foil omitted for unobstructed view of hand and arm position.

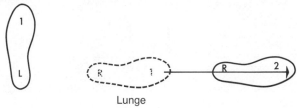

Lunge

**Figure 29.**   Foot pattern of the lunge: (1) first position of feet; (2) second position.

**Figure 30.** The lunge: side view. *Top:* Thrust and beginning of the lunge. *Bottom:* Extended position of the lunge. (Drawn from Castello, H., and Castello, J.: Fencing. © 1960, The Ronald Press Company, New York.)

muscles. The back knee is locked into place and the back foot remains flat on the floor as an anchor. As the back leg is extended, the rear arm is straightened and flung backward so that it makes a 45 degree angle with the body. The palm is facing upward. As in the on guard position, the rear arm should be pulled substantially toward the back so that the profile position of the torso is maintained. The non-foil arm extended position provides some weight as a backward ballast.

To recover backward from the lunge position, push backward from the front foot and return to the on guard position. To recover forward, quickly flex the back leg and bring it to the on guard position. The decision as to whether to recover forward or backward will be based on whether your opponent holds his ground or retreats.

### Advance-lunge

This is a combination of an advance followed by a lunge. Just as the rear foot strikes the floor, the foil arm is extended and followed immediately by the lunge. With practice, a skilled fencer can make the advance flow into the lunge so that they appear to be almost one movement.

## Footwork Drills

1. Advance 5 or 6 times. Can you tap your front toe several times? If not, your weight is too much forward.

2. Advance 8 times, retreat 8 times; advance 4, retreat 4; advance 2, retreat 2; advance 1, retreat 1. Do this entire series 5 times without stopping. Repeat the series 5 times as quickly as possible.

3. Lunge and recover 5 times in succession toward a mirror. Is your on guard position consistent even after the 5 lunges?

4. Lunge, recover, retreat. Repeat 5 times very quickly.

5. Lunge, recover, retreat; lunge, recover, advance. Repeat 5 times without hesitating between the series.

6. Thrust-lunge at a 3 inch square of adhesive tape that you have placed on the wall. How many times out of 10 can you hit it from a lunge initiated from the on guard position? From an advance-lunge?

**Table 3.**  Common Errors in Footwork

| Error | Cause | Correction |
|---|---|---|
| 1. Inability to move forward and backward quickly. | 1A. Taking too large steps while advancing and retreating. | 1A. Practice in front of a mirror; take smaller steps. |
| 2. "Bobbing" up and down during advance and retreat. | 2A. Taking too large steps. | 2A. Take small steps; think of advancing and retreating within a hallway that has a ceiling only $\frac{1}{2}$ inch above your head. |
|  | 2B. Shifting body weight extremely from the front foot to the back foot. | 2B. Keep your weight centered over an imaginary spot between your feet (see Figure 22). |
| 3. Slow recovery to on guard position following lunge. | 3A. Overextension on lunge. | 3A. Keep bulk of weight off front foot; center your weight. |
|  | 3B. Rolling the back foot on its side at the conclusion of the lunge. | 3B. Keep your back foot flat throughout the lunge. |
| 4. Falling off balance in lunge position. | 4A. Front toe pointed inward or outward as it lands. | 4A. Point front toe straight ahead. |
|  | 4B. Knees rotated inward. | 4B. Keep knees over toes; execute lateral stretching exercises if it is difficult to keep knees over toes. |
| 5. Appearance of falling or sagging in the lunge. | 5A. Front foot raised too high off floor when lunging. | 5A. Keep front foot very close to floor throughout lunge and recovery. |
| 6. Undue pain in legs, or "shin-splints," following fencing practice. | 6A. Any of 3, 4, or 5 above. | 6A. Same as 3, 4, or 5 above. |

## Footwork Drills with a Partner

1. Assume the on guard position facing a partner who is also in the on guard position. Advance toward your partner. He should retreat about the same distance so that the measure is maintained. Advance or retreat at random, so that your partner must advance/retreat depending upon what you do. Reverse responsibilities. Are you keeping the measure?

2. Have your partner, facing you but standing on either side of your blade, pull your foil tip forward. As you feel your arm reach full extension, lunge. Practice this until the lunge does not feel "right" unless it occurs at the completion of the full arm extension. Reverse responsibilities.

3. Both fencers assume the on guard position. Your partner should, without notice, retreat. Lunge as soon as he retreats. Try to lunge so quickly that you hit your target before your partner moves his front foot.

4. Have your partner execute a series of advances, retreats, and lunges. You advance, retreat, or lunge depending on what he does. If he retreats, you advance. If he lunges, you retreat. When he recovers from his lunge you can lunge. This type of footwork drill can be continued indefinitely, depending upon how creative you both are. It is challenging to see if you can concoct a footwork pattern that your partner can't follow and, conversely, to attempt to follow any type of pattern that he may present to you.

## Practice Hints

1. Don't be satisfied with just being able to advance, retreat, and lunge. Practice these over and over every day until the on guard position and the footwork are comfortable to you.

2. Have your partner point out to you each time he sees your pommel drooping from your wrist, or the distance between your feet increasing or decreasing.

3. Keep your elbow tucked in so that it will help protect your low outside target.

4. Recover immediately following a lunge. Do not get in the habit of pausing or remaining in the lunge position.

## LINES OF ATTACK

When you are facing an opponent who is in the on guard position (Fig. 31), you will note that you could attack him by passing
your blade on one side or the other of his blade. You could, as well,
attack the high torso or the low torso. To simplify discussions of
attacks as well as defenses, the target is divided by imaginary lines
into four parts that are relative to the position of your opponent's bell
guard. Since they are relative to the bell guard and the bell guard
moves, the lines are obviously not stationary, but mobile. These
are called lines of attack, and a defensive movement called a parry
exists to protect each line. Attacks landing above the hand are in
the high line; those below the hand are low line attacks. The side
of the foil that is toward the back and hips is the outside line, or 6
line. The side of the foil that is in the front part of the torso is the
inside line, or 4 line. This simplifies discussion; for example, an
attack may be described as landing in the inside 4 line. When
opponents' blades are both crossed so that their tips point toward 4
line, they are said to be engaged in 4 line. To engage blades in 6
line, the blades are crossed so that the foils are pointed toward 6
line.

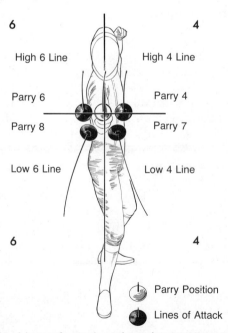

**Figure 31.**  Lines of attack and parries to protect each line.

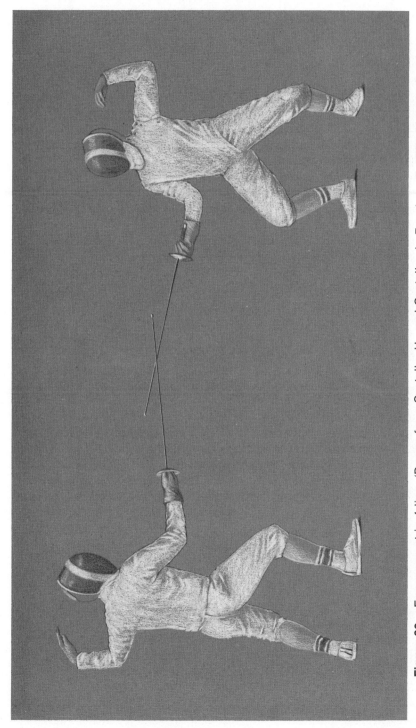

**Figure 32.** Engagement in 4 line. (Drawn from Castello, H., and Castello, J.: Fencing. © 1960, The Ronald Press Company, New York.)

## THE FENCING MEASURE

The fencing measure is the distance that is maintained by two fencers as they bout. It is a distance from which one or both fencers can lunge and hit comfortably with a fully extended foil arm. It is desirable to develop a lunge and maximum agility so that you can fence a greater distance from your opponent than he can from you; i.e., you can hit while maintaining a greater fencing measure than can your opponent. An easy way to find the measure is for Fencer A to assume the on guard position. Fencer B then assumes a fully extended lunge position so that his foil just reaches the torso of A. B then recovers backward to an on guard position, and the distance between A and B will probably be the correct measure. Experienced fencers keep a greater measure between them than do beginners.

When fencers are fencing too close to each other, they are not keeping the measure. This frequently happens when amateurs, who have not developed adequate lunges, fence. It also happens when fencers do not have adequate stamina, and they unconsciously close the distance so that their lunges grow shorter and shorter.

## SIMPLE ATTACKS AND DEFENSES

Attacks and defenses should always be practiced together, for they hardly ever occur in isolation. The attacker must always anticipate a return following his attack, and the defender must think in terms of taking the initiative following a successful defensive manuever. For these reasons, simple attacks and defenses, in addition to compound attacks with more complex defenses, will be discussed and should be practiced together. Also, when practicing, always include drills where you are varying attacks or parries and forcing your opponent to respond to your variations. This will be much more helpful to you than practicing attacks and defenses by rote.

### Simple attacks

An attack is technically initiated by a forward movement of the foil toward the opponent's torso. If you initiate the forward movement first and your foil continues to move forward toward the target, you retain the right-of-way of attack until you either hit target, miss, or have your blade parried. Attacks may be simple or compound, the former being a single movement toward the target and the latter being more than one action toward the target. Whether you plan to execute a simple or complex attack, you must always establish right-of-way first by extending your foil arm forward toward the target.

Simple attacks, even though they are composed of only one action toward the target, can be extremely effective when executed perfectly. An expert fencer, using only simple attacks, can repeatedly penetrate an intermediate fencer's defenses, even if the expert tells the intermediate in advance which attacks he will use. He is able to do this because he executes the attack perfectly and with exquisite timing. Remember, as you learn and practice fencing attacks, that speed and particularly force must acquiesce to timing. Perfect timing is the key to success in penetrating defenses. To execute perfect timing, all simple attacks should be made close to the blade, with quick actions toward the target. The simple attacks described below are the straight thrust, disengage, coupé, and beat-attack.

STRAIGHT THRUST ATTACK. This simple attack is initiated by extending the foil arm quickly and following it almost simultaneously with an explosive lunge. The attack is successful if it is a surprise, or if your lunge allows you to gain more distance than your opponent expects.

DISENGAGE. From an engagement in one line, the blade is extended to the other line by passing it under the opponent's blade and continuing in to hit. Although you change your blade from one side of the opponent's to the other, the movement should be one continuous forward movement. The change of line may be made very simply by relaxing the grip slightly, allowing the tip of the foil to drop and pass very quickly close under the blade. In Figure 33b, you see a diagram of the path of your foil as you look at your opponent. Your foil tip begins on the left side of your opponent's blade and passes under the opponent's blade as you extend your blade forward. You foil tip should hit the opponent's target at $X$ — in high 4 line, just under the bib of his mask.

COUPÉ. This simple attack is similar to the disengage except that the blade is cut sharply over the top of your opponent's foil tip. It is particularly effective if your opponent holds his foil tip low. From the on guard position, bend your wrist upward slightly. This will cause your foil point to raise upward. As soon as it is high enough to clear your opponent's foil tip, extend your foil arm toward the target and lunge. When executed properly, your foil tip enscribes an upside down "V" in the air, so that the upward path is one side of the "V" and the downward path of the foil tip is the other side of the inverted "V" (see Figure 33c). The movement of your blade should be accomplished by bending only your wrist. Do not bend your elbow and raise your forearm upward as you execute the coupé, for as you raise your forearm out of position you expose your lower torso. In addition, when you have your forearm raised, you are in a difficult position from which to parry. By using only wrist flexion to make the coupé, you keep your bell guard in position to protect yourself in the

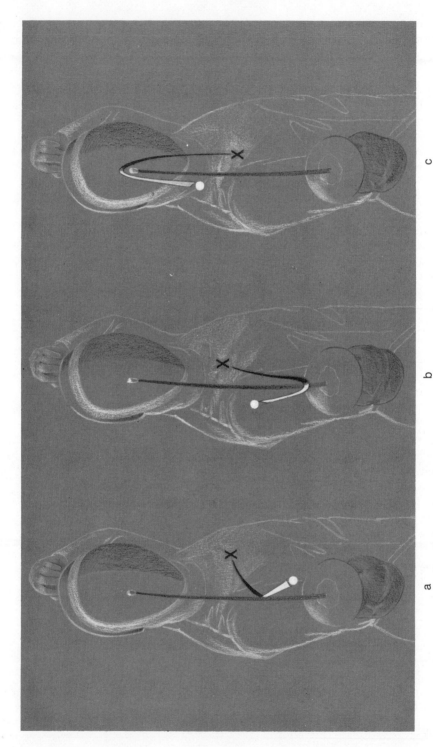

a                    b                    c

**Figure 33.** Simple attacks: (a) beat-attack, (b) disengage, (c) coupé.

event an attack is made upon you in the middle of your coupé. Your aim will also be better if you do not allow your arm and foil tip to wander too far from the on guard position.

BEAT-ATTACK. The beat-attack is almost exactly like the straight thrust attack, except that as the foil arm is extended you spank your opponent's blade crisply and continue your attack. The beat must be with your forte against your opponent's foible, and you must be able to make the beat with only a minimum amount of hand movement. Do not draw your blade back in order to prepare for the beat. Your opponent will predict the beat and evade it. In Figure 33a, note that your foil tip starts on the right side of your opponent's blade. It follows a path straight into the opponent's blade, glances off his blade, and lands on high 4 line target immediately under the bib. The path of your foil does not leave the 4 line throughout this beat-attack. It begins in 4 line and ends in 4 line.

### Simple parries

A parry is a movement of the foil that you make to defend yourself from your opponent's attack. The on guard position is designed so that your bell guard stays in a position that is relatively protective; although your bell guard protects your hand, it certainly

**Table 4.** Common Errors in Executing Simple Attacks

| Error | Cause | Correction |
|---|---|---|
| 1. Blade bends downward or point glances off as it contacts opponent. | 1A. Pommel dangling below wrist or extending above wrist. | 1A. Press pommel against wrist and keep it in line with forearm. |
| | 1B. Attempting to go around the opponent's blade by approaching from the side. | 1B. Keep the fingers up and your arm moving straight forward from your shoulder. |
| 2. Hitting target after completing the lunge. | 2A. Failure to extend the arm prior to the lunge. | 2A. Once you have extended your foil arm, do not bend it until you have hit the target. |
| 3. Missing the target on a beat-attack. | 3A. Blade brought too far out of line in order to execute beat. | 3A. Use only the last three fingers to make the beat. Do not bend your wrist during the beat. |
| 4. Failure to hit on the disengage. | 4A. Disengaging too soon. | 4A. Disengage just as the arm reaches full extension. |
| 5. Hitting the underside of opponent's forearm on the disengage instead of hitting good target. | 5A. Lunging before the arm is extended, thus disengaging too late. | 5A. Complete the disengage before your tip gets to the opponent's bell guard. |
| 6. Failing to hit with the coupé. | 6A. Pausing too long between the upward cut and the downward thrust. | 6A. Make the first part of the cut very short in comparison to the thrust and lunge. |
| 7. Hitting with a flat touch on the shoulder at the conclusion of the coupé. | 7A. Raising the foil tip too high on the upward cut and beginning the lunge too soon. | 7A. Use only the wrist to raise the foil ½ inch above opponent's tip. |

is not large enough to serve as a shield for your entire torso. Nevertheless, your bell guard and forte are all that you have with which to protect yourself. It is necessary, therefore, to move your bell guard to a position that is in front of the part of your target that your opponent is attacking. When you have placed your bell guard squarely in front of one part of your target you have "closed the line." When you move your bell guard to close one line, of course, you are opening another. For this reason it is wise to move into a parry position only when you feel certain that your opponent is attacking you at that particular place. Following a parry, you should return immediately to the on guard position, from which you may move with equal ease to protect any part of your target.

Parries may be made either by a movement that is primarily a blocking type of movement or by a deflecting type of movement. A blocking type of parry is one in which you contact, with your forte, your opponent's foible and middle blade and push them sideways away from your target. This sounds difficult to do, but it is not. If your foil arm is in the proper on guard position, a blocking type of parry is simply a matter of moving your bell guard an inch or two in the desired direction. You also have a great leverage advantage when you parry, for you are using your bell guard and the strong part of your blade against your opponent's foible. The deflecting type of parry is also called a beat parry. The beat parry is a manuever in which you "spank" or sharply tap your opponent's blade hard enough so that it is deflected away from the target. The beat parry is used more frequently by fencers, as it is a natural and instinctive type of defensive movement. The beat should not cover much distance, however, for a large preparatory movement and a big follow-through would take your own blade out of line. If the attack is a simple attack, the beat parry need only be strong enough to deflect the blade momentarily from the target. Blocking and beating are only the types of movement used as parries; however, they are not the names of the parries. The simple parries are called parries 4 and 6, and 7 and 8.

PARRIES 4 AND 6.    Inasmuch as most attacks are terminated in high 4 or 6 line, most of them may be defended by the simple parries 4 and 6. These parries are named according to the part of the target they protect, and they are executed by making very small horizontal movements of the bell guard and forte. Because of this horizontal movement they are also called lateral parries 4 and 6.

Parry 4, a blocking type of parry, is made by moving the bell guard slightly to the left. Your hand and elbow remain in the same position as in the on guard position, with the pommel next to the wrist and the palm up. Your foil tip must move with your bell guard movement slightly to the left, so that you maintain the straight line of your elbow, blade, and tip. If you move your bell guard but leave your tip pointing at your opponent's target, you will have to bend your wrist or let your pommel drift away from your wrist. Either of these two actions eliminates your leverage advantage. Your leverage comes from contacting or "catching" your opponent's foible with your bell guard and forte, and pushing the foible away. Remember that if you keep your foil elbow approximately 6 inches away from your body, then your bell guard is a considerable distance away from your body. Therefore, it only takes a slight lateral movement at the bell guard to cause a larger displacement of your opponent's foil tip by the time it arrives near the target.

Parry 6 is made essentially as parry 4 except that it is moved in the opposite direction. The bell guard is moved slightly to your right to close your 6 line. Allow your point to move slightly to the right also, but try to keep it pointing at some part of the target, even if it is just the edge of your opponent's target.

If you wish to make a deflecting type of parry 4 or 6, simply spank with your forte the opponent's foible or middle blade as it approaches the vicinity of your bell guard. A spank to the left is a beat parry of 4, and a spank to the right is a beat parry of 6.

PARRIES 7 AND 8. These parries are also simple parries, although somewhat more blade movement is required. Parry 7 protects the low inside or 7 line. Parry 8 protects the low outside or 8 line. To execute a parry 7 sharply whip your blade in a clockwise arc so that your foil tip moves quickly from pointing at your opponent's chest to pointing at a place just to the left and above your opponent's forward knee. This clockwise motion of your blade may also be described as drawing in the air an imaginary backward letter C. The arc that your blade makes enables you to find your opponent's blade, no matter how low it is, and deflect it from the target. Parry 8 is the reverse of parry 7. The blade is moved counterclockwise, stopping when the foil tip is pointing just to the inside of your opponent's knee. Parry 8 may be described as making a letter C in the air with your foil tip. In both parries 7 and 8, the hand does not move downward; only the foil tip and blade move downward.

## Simple Attack and Defense Drills

1. Fencer A advances on B with 10 very quick advances. Fencer B, in response, retreats 10 times. A then retreats 10 while B advances. At the conclusion of these, check to see if the two of you have kept the measure.

2. Attack 5 times in 4 line with a straight thrust attack. Attack 5 times in 6 line. Make the blade bend slightly each time you hit target. Repeat with your partner parrying each of the attacks.

**Table 5.** Common Errors in Executing Simple Parries

| Error | Cause | Correction |
|---|---|---|
| 1. Beating your opponent's blade into your legs while parrying 4. | 1A. Parrying downward when using parry 4. | 1A. Movement of your parry 4 should be horizontal, not downward. |
| 2. Sliding or swishing sound of the blades throughout an attack and parry. | 2A. Anticipation of attack by defender. | 2A. Wait until you know the attack is really an attack and not just a feint. |
|  | 2B. Hesitation of lunge following extension by attacker. | 2B. Follow the extension immediately with a lunge. |
| 3. Opponent's blade overpowers parry 4 or 6 and hits in spite of the parry. | 3A. Failure to move bell guard horizontally and completely to the edge of your target. | 3A. Be sure your elbow is in and that the line from your elbow to the tip of your foil is straight. |
|  | 3B. Pommel leaves wrist allowing the "break" in the foilarm defense. | 3B. Press pommel firmly against the wrist throughout the parry. |

3. Beat-attack 5 times in 4 line. Repeat with your partner parrying.

4. Have your partner parry your beat-attack some of the time but not every time. You may find that when your partner unexpectedly does not parry, you nevertheless fail to hit. If this happens, you will know that you are not executing your attack properly because you most certainly should hit if your partner fails to parry.

5. Vary a straight thrust attack with a beat-attack. Partner attempts parries.

6. Vary the lines of attack with your partner parrying.

7. Vary a straight thrust attack with the disengage attack. If each is executed properly, and if you vary them cleverly, you should hit on almost every attack even though your partner is attempting to parry.

8. Vary the coupé attack with the straight thrust. If you cleverly vary these, your opponent will never know which attack is coming and you will be able to hit many times, in spite of the fact that your opponent knows you will use only one of two attacks.

9. Thrust high in 6 line but drop your point to hit in low 6. Your partner will practice parry 8. Thrust high in 4 line but drop your point to attack the low inside line. Your partner will practice parry 7.

## Practice Hints

1. In simple attacks, keep your blade close to your opponent's and thrust directly to the nearest target available.

2. Think of the beat in the beat-attack as a glancing blow that is executed on the way in as you thrust, i.e., as a glancing blow as you extend.

3. Make your disengages with your arm in full extension and as close to your opponent's blade as you can keep your blade without touching his.

4. Remember that the smaller the movement you make, the less time it takes; also, the shortest distance between two points is a straight line. Every time you raise or lower your foil tip above or below the target you are lengthening the amount of time it will take you to hit.

5. Always parry with the strong part of your blade in combination with your bell guard. If you use these strong segments of your blade against your opponent's foible or middle blade, and if you keep your pommel next to your wrist, no opponent can overpower your parries.

6. When parrying, always maintain your elbow about 6 inches away from your body. If you miss your first parry, the 6 inches gives you time and space to pull your hand back toward your body to parry again.

7. Keep your bell guard in the on guard position and use only wrist flexion to coupé. This way, if your opponent suddenly attacks you in the middle of your coupé you can always parry.

## THE RIPOSTE

The riposte is such an important part of fencing that you should learn it along with your simplest defenses. The riposte should, in fact, be an instinctive follow-through of every parry you make. Basically, the riposte is regaining the right-of-way by initiating a return attack as soon as you have successfully parried. Just as attacks may be simple or complex, so are ripostes categorized as simple (direct), indirect, and compound. A riposte can be extremely effective if you initiate it before your opponent has time to recover. He would thus be in the position of having to defend himself while still in the lunge position or while returning to the on guard position.

### Simple (direct) riposte

From the parry position of 4 or 6, simply extend your tip or foil arm to hit in the same line. Let your tip move first and aim it at the closest part of your opponent's target. If you are quick enough to hit before your opponent can return to his on guard position, you will be able to execute the simple riposte with only an arm extension. If you are slower, you may have to follow the arm extension with a lunge. Naturally, it is desirable to riposte with only the arm extension since it is faster and requires less energy. Your riposte will be lightning quick if you have left your point in line and moved your bell guard little on the parry.

### Indirect and compound riposte

To execute an indirect riposte from the parry position of 4 or 6, disengage or coupé to extend your foil and hit in the line opposite that to which the attack was made. The compound riposte involves more than one action toward the target. Inasmuch as a riposte is a retaking of the attack, any compound attack may be utilized as a riposte. Compound attacks are discussed in this chapter, and their uses as ripostes are discussed in Chapter 7, Advanced Techniques.

## Riposte Drills

1. Fencer A attacks with a straight thrust lunge in 4 line 5 times. Fencer B should parry and riposte, each time hitting in his opponent's 4 line. Repeat the drill in 6 line.

2. Fencer A attacks in either 4 or 6 line. B parries and ripostes. Fencer A should vary the attacks so that B cannot predict the line in which the attack will come.

**Table 6.** Common Errors in Executing a Riposte

| Error | Cause | Correction |
|---|---|---|
| 1. Riposte is short of the target. | 1A. Arm is not fully extended. | 1A. Extend the arm until it is straight and lean forward slightly. |
| | 1B. Failing to aim at the opponent's shoulder or other close part of the target. | 1B. Put your point in line first and then move it toward the closest part of the target. |
| | 1C. Hesitating at the conclusion of the arm extension. | 1C. Follow the arm extension immediately with a lunge if the point has not landed on the extension. |
| 2. Riposte fails to hit. | 2A. Riposte is parried. | 2A. Riposte immediately following parry. |
| | 2B. Hesitating after parry. | 2B. Move from the parry position directly to the arm extension; do not return to the on guard position before riposting. |
| | 2C. Parry consumes too much time. | 2C. Leave the bell guard in the on guard position as you parry, and extend from the parry position. |
| 3. Finding your blade extending beyond your opponent's back or front target, so that you have to withdraw your blade in order to place it on target. | 3A. Leaning forward with your body or lunging before your arm extension. | 3A. Lunge only after you feel your arm reach full extension. |

3. Fencer A attacks in either 4 or 6 line. B parries, ripostes, and retreats. Repeat 4 times.

4. Fencer A attacks in 4 line. B parries and ripostes, but A then parries the riposte and hits B. Repeat 4 times.

5. Fencer A initiates a straight attack. B parries and ripostes, A parries the riposte, B parries A's riposte, A parries the riposte, and hits B. This drill may be continued for any number of parry-riposte combinations, but at some point (preferably when B determines the action to be getting arhythmic) B should fail to parry and let A terminate the drill by hitting. Many times even though B does not parry, A does not hit but finds his blade wandering about in space. This is a dramatic signal to A that he has not been driving his point directly and forcefully toward the target. This kind of practice is wasted.

6. Fencer A attacks with a simple attack and immediately recovers and retreats; B parries, and ripostes with a lunge. Repeat 4 times.

## Practice Hints

1. Do not hesitate following the parry. Riposte immediately.

2. Watch your distance and lunge only when necessary.

3. Practice a variety of ripostes; refrain from using the same one habitually.

4. If your riposte seems to fall short when you merely extend your arm, check your opponent's lunge distance to see if he could hit you had you not parried. Frequently in drill situations attackers get lazy and fail to lunge deep enough to hit. Generally if your opponent attacks deep enough to hit you with an attack, you can reach him with a fast riposte without lunging.

## COMPOUND ATTACKS AND COUNTER PARRIES

Compound attacks, also called composed attacks, are comprised of more than one movement toward the target. The initial movement may be a feint or a preparatory action upon the blade. A feint is an extension of the arm and foil into an open line. The purpose of the feint is to provoke a parry by making your opponent believe you are attacking in that line. If a compound attack is initiated first, it will carry right-of-way throughout the attack unless the blade is caught or found by the opponent in the middle of the attack. It is, therefore, important that each action of a compound attack be "believable" to

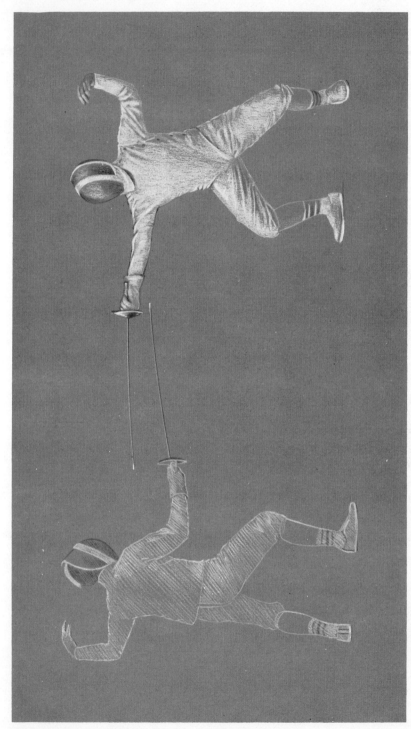

**Figure 34.** The feint. (Drawn from Castello, H., and Castello, J.: Fencing. © 1960, The Ronald Press Company, New York.)

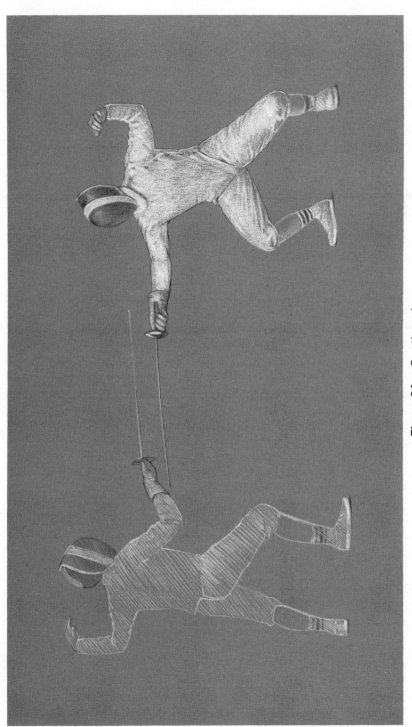

**Figure 34.**  *Continued.*

the opponent, so that he will follow the actions and thus be still following on the final action at which time he is hit. The objective, then, of compound attacks is to feint an attack into an open line and deceive the opponent's parry in that line so that you may hit in the originally closed line.

All compound attacks must be made subtly, with your blade close to your opponent's and always in direct line with this target. Any wild feints or beats upon the blade in which your foil is carried far afield from your opponent are easily detected and should be avoided, since it takes you much more time to bring your foil back into the line of attack. Some good compound attacks to begin learning include the feint-disengage, beat-disengage, double-disengage, and coupé-disengage.

## Compound attacks

FEINT-DISENGAGE. Thrust your arm forcefully toward your opponent's target in an open line. If your thrust is believable — that is, if your opponent believes that you are going to follow that extension with a lunge in that line — he will parry. As his bell guard moves across his target in an attempt to find your blade, drop your foil tip about 1 inch and let it slip under your opponent's forte. Your lunge should begin as your tip is directly under your opponent's forte. With practice the lunge become synchronous with the disengage, and the disengage becomes cleanly timed to the opponent's parry.

BEAT-DISENGAGE. The beat is a sharp spank upon the blade. It is human nature to press back against a beat upon your weapon; the beat therefore tends to draw a parry sometimes more effectively than a feint. When used sparingly the beat is very effective. When used continuously it becomes a waste of time.

In an open line, beat your opponent's blade sharply and extend your foil forcefully. As the opponent's guard is moving across to parry, slip your tip deftly under your opponent's forte and lunge. Do not bend your extended elbow once your attack has begun.

DOUBLE-DISENGAGE. From a closed line, disengage and thrust simultaneously into the open line. If done unexpectedly and forcefully, this should draw a self defensive reaction from your opponent in the form of a parry. As the parry is moving across to close or protect that line, slip back under to the original line and lunge. With practice the second disengage and lunge become almost simultaneous.

COUPÉ-DISENGAGE. Cut your blade, as in a simple coupé, over your opponent's blade from a closed line to an open one and thrust vigorously. As the opponent parries, evade the parry with a disengage and lunge. The deeper into your opponent's target you can thrust, and the longer you can hold the thrust before disengaging, the higher your chances are of hitting. This attack must look exactly like a simple coupé right up until you disengage. Make your opponent commit himself with a parry before you initiate your disengage.

## Drills for Compound Attacks

1. Fencer A feints in high 4 line. Fencer B parries in 4. With the initiation of B's movement, A disengages and lunges in 6 line.

2. Repeat drill 1, but B should parry at random; that is, sometimes B parries in 4 and other times he deliberately remains motionless. If the parry does occur, A should disengage.

3. Same as in drill 2 except that the attack is initiated by a beat-thrust. If a parry occurs, disengage and attack in the opening line. If not, continue in with a beat-attack.

4. Vary a disengage with a double-disengage. Practice "setting up" your opponent for a double-disengage by attacking in the same line several times. For instance, disengage from 4 to 6 line 3 or 4 times. On the next attack, double-disengage.

**Table 7.** Common Errors in Making Compound Attacks

| Error | Cause | Correction |
|---|---|---|
| 1. Failure to hit with the feint-disengage. | 1A. Feint is not believable. | 1A. Make the feint with emphasis, deep in the open line; keep your blade close to your opponent's. |
| | 1B. Disengage is delayed following the feint. | 1B. Disengage the moment your opponent's blade begins to move in response to the feint. |
| 2. Failure to complete the beat-disengage; blade becomes entangled in your opponent's arm. | 2A. Lunge is initiated before the disengage. | 2A. Lunge only as your tip drops under your opponent's forte; keep your arm and foil high and parallel with the floor. |
| 3. Failure to hit with a double-disengage. | 3A. Disengages are too wide and too large. | 3A. Make disengages by alternately contracting and relaxing the last three fingers of the grip. |
| | 3B. First disengage is made out of distance and is not threatening. | 3B. Make the first disengage deep into the opponent's space, at least so that your tip is almost to your opponent's bell guard. |
| | 3C. Failure to pause on the first disengage long enough to provoke a parry from your opponent. | 3C. Begin second disengage only after your opponent's parry is initiated. |
| 4. Failure to hit on the coupé-disengage. | 4A. Failure to allow the blade to pause and move forward slightly at the end of the cut before disengaging. | 4A. Wait until the parry for the cut-thrust is started before disengaging. |

5. Same as in drill 4, but use the coupé. Practice attacking with the coupé from 4 to 6 line and from 6 to 4 line.

## Practice Hints

1. Your point should always lead in any attack.

2. When making a compound attack, never bend your arm in the middle of the attack. When this happens you lose right-of-way.

3. Regardless of the number of actions in a compound attack, your point should continually move forward in a steady continuous motion.

4. Your final action should occur in a line that is being opened, rather than one that is being closed.

5. Any feint that you execute must provoke a parry from your opponent. If it does not, further actions of a compound attack are useless.

6. Leave your feint in the open line as long as is necessary for the opponent to see it and to begin his parry. A compound attack that is completed with blinding speed against a slow reactor will probably be parried successfully with a simple parry because a slower fencer will not even see or react to all of the speedy feints.

7. Emphasize the first feint of a series of feints.

### Counter parries

The counter parries 4 and 6 are also called circular parries. When your opponent leaves your closed line by disengaging, you may locate his blade again by making a full circle with yours. Thus, if your 6 line is closed and your opponent leaves 6, you may circle your blade under his and push his blade back into the line of 6 again. You could also counter parry 6 from a closed 4 line. Actually the term "circular" parry is a bit misleading, because the parry is much faster when it is executed with so little movement that the foil tip, rather than making a circle, describes a semi-"V" in the air. Your bell guard remains in almost the same position, with perhaps a slight horizontal movement toward the line you are closing. Usually a counter parry is easier to learn and more effective if you retreat once as you execute it. The counter parry is very effective, because it enables you to regain a defense when you have lost your opponent's blade; even if you are not able to conclude the action successfully with a parry, sometimes the counter parry will destroy the timing of your opponent or knock his blade from its intended course long enough for you to retreat and recover.

Counter parries may, of course, be combined with the simple

parries, but this will be discussed in Chapter 7, Advanced Techniques. You should never get in the habit of always making one kind of parry, such as a simple 4 and 6 or counter parries. Your opponent will then be able to predict your actions and when he can predict your parries he can generally penetrate them.

## Drills for Counter Parries

1. Fencer A disengages from 6 to 4 and attacks. Fencer B uses the counter parry 6. Repeat 5 times. Repeat the drill using a disengage from 4 to 6 and using the counter parry 4.

2. Repeat drill 1, but B alternates using a simple parry of 4 or 6 with a counter parry.

3. Fencer A varies a thrust attack with a disengage. B partially responds to A's thrust in 4 line. When B begins the straight parry, A disengages, whereupon B immediately responds with counter parry 4. Alternate lines. The emphasis of this drill is for A to make B "honest." Sometimes A should continue in with the straight thrust into 4 line, in which case B's response should be the simply parry 4. If B continues into a counter parry which is unnecessary, it will be very obvious. Conversely, if A disengages and B is expecting only the straight thrust, B will be hit in 6 line.

**Table 8.** Common Errors in Executing Counter Parries

| Error | Cause | Correction |
|---|---|---|
| 1. Slow and ineffective counter parries. | 1A. Moving the blade in large circles. | 1A. Keep the bell guard in approximately the same position, moving it horizontally to the closed position at the conclusion of your bladework. |
| | 1B. Enscribing a circle in the air instead of a "V" with the tip of the foil. | 1B. Think of the counter parries as "V"s rather than circles; think of them as terminating in the simple parries of 4 and 6. |
| | 1C. Moving the blade the wrong direction. | 1C. Practice until the direction of the counter parry is automatic; think of your blade as following or going in the same direction as your opponent's. |
| 2. Being hit in spite of executing a correct counter parry. | 2A. Attempting to parry your opponent's forte with your foible. | 2A. Start the counter parry only when you are sure your opponent is disengaging. |
| | 2B. Failing to complete counter parry before you are hit. | 2B. Retreat with the counter parry; the retreat will gain you time. |

## Practice Hints

1. Try to respond only to blade actions that seem to be real attacks; do not respond to wild feints or actions directed to areas other than your target.

2. Make each movement a definite action terminating in a distinct parry which closes a line.

3. Learn to accompany parries with the retreat.

4. As soon as you no longer have to worry about the direction of the counter parry, begin habitually to accompany it with a simple riposte.

## SAFETY IN FENCING

Fencing is not a dangerous sport if elementary rules of safety are observed. Most injuries to fencers are blisters of the hands and feet and pulled or strained muscles. Ankles are sometimes sprained. You can avoid almost all injuries if you observe these simple safety rules, both in practice and in tournaments.

1. Condition yourself physically before the competitive fencing season and stay in condition. Fencing tournaments, more often than not, start early in the morning and do not terminate until late evening. If you are well conditioned, you may avoid injuries attributable to fatigue in the late hours of a tournament.

2. Warm up before fencing a bout. Include some vigorous jumping, bending, and stretching exercises.

3. Use equipment that is in good repair; a defective blade can be fatal.

4. Tuck your foil-arm sleeve under your glove. If the sleeve is outside the glove, the opponent's foil blade might be driven up your sleeve and may cut the forearm.

5. Wear thick, rubber-soled, good fitting shoes and thick socks when you fence.

6. Keep the fencing strip and surrounding areas free of clothing and fencing equipment. Foils or masks lying near a fencing strip might inadvertently trip a fencer.

7. Always use your own equipment.

## CHAPTER 5

# RULES AND
# OFFICIATING

## RULES

Official fencing competition is governed by the rules adopted and published by the Amateur Fencers League of America (AFLA). The AFLA has adopted almost identically the rules set forward by the Federation International d'Escrime (FIE). Since FIE rules are used almost everywhere, fencing competitions—unlike many competitions in other sports—are consistent in rules whether the fencing is at the elementary, high school, college, or community level anywhere in the world. It is comforting to know that, having mastered the rules as published in the AFLA *Fencing Rules and Manual,* you will understand the rules—with perhaps slight local modifications—governing whatever competitions you may attend. The rules presented in this book are general guidelines for the beginner, who might be intimidated by the myriad of details and complexities presented to the reader of the official rules. In the event that fencing captivates you to the point that you elect to continue lessons and compete, you should purchase an official handbook of the rules from
Amateur Fencers League of America
33 62nd Street
West New York, N. J. 07093

### Field of play

The regulation fencing strip is 39 feet, 4 inches long and 5 feet 11 inches wide, with a minimum of 5 feet of "run back" room behind the end line. Dimensions converted from the FIE metric system and rounded to the nearest inch are shown in Figure 35.

### Equipment

Every fencer who crosses blades with another should be fully equipped with a regulation weapon and adequate uniform as de-

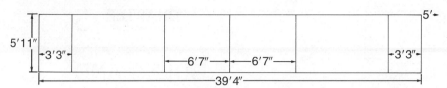

**Figure 35.** Regulation fencing strip.

scribed in Chapter 1. This includes a mask with bib, glove, fencing jacket, and foil. A martingale is required in competitions where electric equipment is not used.

### The target

The foil target consists of the torso, excluding the arms. The bib of the mask is not valid target area, but it should be remembered that the back is good target. Hits that are made in off-target areas are counted as touches if the fencer, by contorting his body into abnormal positions, has substituted an off-target area for valid target area.

### The touch

Touches are awarded on the basis of materiality and priority of the hit. Only those hits that arrive on valid target as the conclusion of a thrusting motion are counted. Hits which land on off-target areas are not counted as touches, but they stop action and nullify any touch that follows.

MATERIALITY. The materiality of the touch is determined by evaluating whether the point of the foil actually contacts the opponent, and determining whether the landing site is on or off target. In addition, the directness of the thrust initiating the hit is evaluated. Any movement classified as a sideward, downward, or upward action which results in a slap, slide, flat or laid-on hit is not counted.

PRIORITY OF THE HIT. When only one fencer is hit, priority of the touch is of no consequence. When both fencers hit either simultaneously or nearly simultaneously, however, the matter is resolved by determining whose touch has priority. The fencer whose hit is the result of a correctly executed attack properly made within the fencing phrase has priority. He has established right-of-way, the phrase referring to the fact that any correctly executed attack must be parried or completely avoided before the non-attacker may rejoin.

Once a fencer has initiated an attack, usually by thrusting, his opponent is obligated to parry before he may return the attack. There are two exceptions to this rule. First, if the attacker is attempting to find, or deflect, the blade of his opponent and is evaded, the right-of-way passes to the opponent. Second, if the attacker makes a compound attack composed of so many movements that the defender is able to stop-hit the attacker one full action before the arrival of the attack, the hit is awarded in this case against the attacker. A stop hit is an extension of the foil arm and blade that is made into an attack. It has no right-of-way, but in the exception mentioned above, the stop hit lands on target first. Stop hits are difficult to achieve, however, and the beginning fencer would do well to postpone these until well-executed attacks with right-of-way take on the character of reflex action.

*The fencer who is attacked and hit is counted as being touched when*

1. He makes a stop hit against a simple attack.
2. He fails to parry or parries inadequately.
3. He pauses momentarily following an adequate parry.
4. He makes a stop hit during a composite attack but fails to hit in time.

*The fencer who attacks and is hit is counted as touched when*

1. He initiates an attack against a straight arm with point in line and fails to deflect the blade.
2. He attempts to envelop the opponent's blade, fails, but continues the attack anyway.
3. He allows the opponent to find the blade during his composite attack, and fails to parry the opponent's immediate riposte.
4. He pauses at any time during a composite attack and the opponent stop-hits while he continues his attack.
5. He is hit by a stop hit just prior to the final movement of his compound attack.

*Neither fencer is counted as touched when*

1. The hit with priority is an off-target hit.
2. Both fencers hit simultaneously and neither fencer has right-of-way. This usually occurs when both fencers are at fault; the attacker may not have initiated the attack correctly or may have hesitated, and the defender may have delayed or failed to parry or may have been slow to stop-hit.
3. On rare occasions, both fencers correctly initiate attacks and hit simultaneously.

*The fencing action is always stopped immediately by the director when*

1. A judge raises his hand.
2. A fencer runs off the strip, either across side or end lines.
3. The fencers reverse positions on the strip in the middle of a fencing phrase.
4. The fencers become stalemated in a corps à corps; that is, the fencers' bell guards are locked or pressed together and neither fencer will retreat.

5. The timekeeper indicates the time period of the bout has terminated.

### Postion on the strip and line regulations

FENCING POSITION.   The fencer whose name is first called positions himself to the right of the director. This places the fencer so that the front part of his torso is facing the director. Conversely, the director looks at the back side of the fencer to his left. The fencing schedule is constructed so that all fencers in the competition have the opportunity of being positioned to the right of the director. An exception to this rule of position is made in the event one of the fencers is left-handed and is called first. If the left-hander placed himself on the right of the director, and the right-hander placed himself to the left of the director, then the director would be looking at both of their backs. It is extremely difficult for the director to see the bladework from this point of view, so it is customary for the left-handed fencer to place himself on the director's left, whether his name is called first or second.

The fencers assume a position of on guard behind the on guard line when the director says "On Guard." The director will then say, "Ready," and upon receiving an affirmative reply from both fencers will then say "Fence" Following the directive "Fence," either fencer may initiate an attack. The bout must stop when the director says "Halt," and if a fencer stops prior to this command and is hit in the process, the touch is awarded against him. However, hits made after the command "Halt" are not counted as touches. After each touch is awarded, the fencers are put on guard at the on guard line. If a fencing phrase is halted but no touch is awarded, the fencers are put on guard by the director wherever the action was stopped, except in cases of line violations as discussed below. This procedure allows a fencer who has gained ground by pushing his opponent back to his own end line, to maintain that advantage in the event the action was interrupted when no touch is awarded. A fencer who is to fence the next bout is "on deck."

EXCHANGING POSITIONS.   Fencers exchange positions when one of them has received half the maximum number of hits that he can receive. When a left-hander fences a right-hander, however, the judges rather than the fencers change sides (Fig. 36). Exchanging positions is not allowed during the fencing phrase. In the event fencers inadvertently exchange positions, the action is halted and the fencers are put on guard as they were when the reversing action occurred.

END LINE VIOLATIONS.   When a fencer is pushed back so that both feet retreat past the end line, the director halts the bout imme-

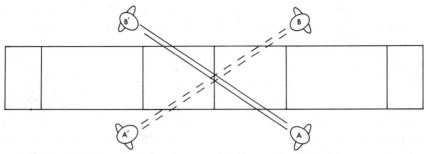

**Figure 36.** Change of judges' positions midway in a right-hander *vs.* left-hander bout; fencers do not change sides.

diately and counts a touch against him, *provided* he has been previously warned. A warning is provided

1. When a fencer's rear foot touches the warning line the first time.

2. When a warned fencer touches the warning line again after regaining a position so that his front foot touches his on guard line.

3. When the fencer is driven beyond the end line with both feet in a flurry of bladework so rapid that a warning was not possible. In this special case, an immediate riposte or stop hit by the retreating fencer will be valid even if both feet have crossed the end line.

When a competitor crosses the end line with both feet after having been warned he cannot score a touch against his attacker. If the attacker hits, however, it is valid provided it is made as a part of the blade movement that was occurring as the defender crossed the end line.

SIDE LINE VIOLATIONS. When a fencer crosses one of the side lines of the strip with both feet, he is penalized by having to resume his on guard position a distance of 3 feet, 3 inches toward his own end line from the location of the violation. If this penalty places both his feet beyond the end line, a touch is counted against him—provided he has been previously warned. The competitor who is crossing the side line may be touched by the fencer remaining on the strip, providing that the hit occurs as part of the blade movement occurring as the line violation was made.

### Bout duration

A fencing bout terminates for men when five touches or six minutes have occurred, whichever is first; for women the bout terminates when four touches or five minutes occur. The clock is started each time the director says "Fence," and stopped at each "Halt." The fencing bout does not, therefore, include the deliberation and decision-making time of the director and the jury. Fencers are not permitted to see the official clock; they are, however, advised by the director when only one minute remains in the bout.

### Officials and officiating

THE DIRECTOR.   The director has complete control of the fencing bout. He directs the bout, controls equipment, supervises all judges, scores, and timers, awards touches, penalizes faults, and otherwise maintains order. He places himself a distance from the strip that is approximately equidistant from the fencers (see Fig. 37). The director must be far enough away from the strip that he can see the raised hand of any judge with his peripheral vision. When a judge raises his arm, the director immediately calls "Halt." He then polls the jury to determine the materiality of the hit. Although the director has $1\frac{1}{2}$ votes and may vote on the materiality of the hit, his primary responsibility is to determine priority. The jury is primarily responsible for determining materiality of a hit, but the director alone determines priority.

Generally, the director verbally reconstructs the last fencing phrase prior to the "Halt" and polls the two judges observing the action that had right-of-way. In the event that this action did not result in a hit, the director polls the two judges who observed the fencing action which followed. This procedure is followed until validity of a hit is established, or until the source of right-of-way or timing of the actions can no longer be deciphered by the director. In this latter case, the director does not award a touch, and the action is resumed.

THE JURY.   The jury is composed of four judges, two who scrutinize the target of one fencer and two who observe the other. The judges position themselves approximately three feet to the side and three feet behind each fencer (Fig. 37). The judges on the director's right watch the fencers on the director's left; the remaining judges observe the other competitor. The judge's primary responsibility is to determine the materiality of a hit. A judge does not determine right-of-way, nor does he ever stop a bout except in the case of injury. When a judge sees a hit, he raises his hand instantly and vigorously. He must then wait to be polled by the director. There are times when the director may not ask for his vote, such as if the hit that he saw is the result of a stop hit that was out of order.

A judge has one vote, and may reply in one of four ways:

*Yes*—the hit landed directly on valid target and was the result of a thrusting type movement;

*Yes, but off-target*—the hit landed directly on invalid target and was the result of a thrusting type movement;

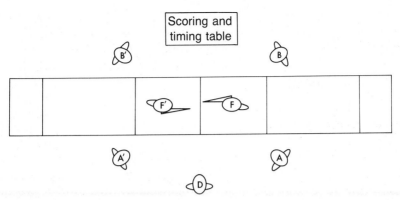

**Figure 37.** Positions of fencers, judges, and director at the beginning of the bout. Judges A and B observe the target of F′, while A′ and B′ observe the target of F.

*No* — the point did not land, or the contact was a result of a slap, slide, flat, or laid-on contact;

*Abstain* — the judge does not vote; this usually happens when the judge's view is obstructed by the fencer's arm or turned body.

THE DIRECTOR'S DECISION. The director has 1½ votes regarding materiality of a hit, and judges each have one vote. The decision of materiality of a hit is a matter only of adding the votes. Examples of possible outcomes are listed in Table 9. It may be seen that the director can outvote one judge, but if the judges agree, they can outvote the director. The director usually doesn't vote at all except in cases where he feels one judge is in error. When he votes, he votes last. Many directors are loath to break a tie, feeling that if the judges disagree there is doubt enough to declare the action "Doubtful." Inasmuch as directors generally are watching the blades between the fencers while concentrating on the phrasing of the attacks, they are not in as good a position to determine materiality of a hit as are the judges assigned to that target. The director, after polling the judges' and his own votes and determining right-of-way, makes his decision

**Table 9.**

| Judge A | Judge B | Director | Voting | Yes | Yes, Off-Target | No | Final Decision |
|---------|---------|----------|--------|-----|-----------------|-----|----------------|
| Yes | Yes | Abstain | 1-1-0 | 1+1=2 | | | Valid |
| Yes | No | Abstain | 1-1-0 | 1 | | 1 | Doubtful |
| Yes | No | Yes | 1-1-1½ | 1+1½=2½ | | 1 | Yes |
| Yes | Yes | No | 1-1-1½ | 1+1=2 | | 1½ | Yes |
| Yes | Off-T | Abstain | 1-1-0 | 1 | 1 | | Doubtful |
| Yes | Abstain | Off-T | 1-0-1½ | 1 | 1½ | | Off-Target |
| No | Off-T | Yes | 1-1-1½ | 1½ | 1 | 1 | Doubtful |

regarding the award of a touch. He does this by calling out the touch against the fencer's name, i.e., "Touch against Mr. Jones." For example, when you hear the score Jones 3-2, you know that Jones has three touches against him and he is, therefore, trailing in the bout.

## SCORING

The touches scored against each competitor are recorded on a score sheet such as that shown in Figure 38. This score sheet is the record of a hypothetical female competition, so that only 4 touches are tallied in the boxes showing each competitor's defeat. If this score sheet had been that recorded for a male competition, each box showing a D would have 5 touches tallied.

The competitors' names are listed on the score sheet, and they are assigned the number by their name. The column labeled "5 Fencers" that is circled at the bottom of the score sheet indicates that this was a pool of five fencers. The first pair of numbers shows that Fencer 1, Burdeshaw, fenced 2, Dalton, first, and that Burdeshaw started fencing on the director's right. Fencers follow the order indicated by the paired numbers. This order is planned, so that competitors rarely have to fence twice in succession. Before the two fencers begin fencing, the scorer draws a horizontal line across the box that is in each fencer's row and her opponent's column. Each touch that is recorded against a competitor is recorded as a small vertical tally mark in the upper half of her box. For instance, when Burdeshaw fences Dalton, a horizontal line is drawn across the box that is in Burdeshaw's row (1) and Dalton's column (2). To discover how Burdeshaw fared in her bout with Dalton, read across Burdeshaw's row. You can see that she not only defeated Dalton, but Dalton did not score a single touch against her. If you wish to determine the outcome of the bout from Dalton's point of view, look in Dalton's row (2) under Burdeshaw's column (1). You see the 4 touches that Burdeshaw scored against Dalton tallied in the upper half of the box, and a D in the lower half, indicating that she lost the bout.

When four touches are recorded against a female competitor, as is the case in the first column for Dalton, a D (defeat) is recorded in the lower half of the box. A V (victory) is recorded in the winner's box—in this case, Burdeshaw's. This shows that Dalton lost to Burdeshaw 4-0. By reading across the boxes on Dalton's row, you can tell exactly what happened to Dalton in the competition. She was defeated 4-0 by Burdeshaw, and 4-2 by Hewatt, but she defeated Lovett 4-3 and Slacks 4-2.

The winner of the pool is the competitor with the most victories.

Fencing Score Sheet

COMPETITION _Texas Invitational_ DATE _5-15-71_
ROUND _Semifinal_ DIRECTOR _Thompson_

| NAMES | NO | 1 | 2 | 3 | 4 | 5 | Touches Against | V | D | Place |
|-------|----|----|----|----|----|----|----------------|---|---|-------|
| Burdeshaw | 1 | | $\frac{0}{V}$ | $\frac{0}{V}$ | $\frac{11}{V}$ | $\frac{1111}{D}$ | | 3 | 1 | 1 — up |
| Dalton | 2 | $\frac{1111}{D}$ | | $\frac{1111}{D}$ | $\frac{111}{V}$ | $\frac{11}{V}$ | 13 | 2 | 2 | 4 |
| Hewatt | 3 | $\frac{1111}{D}$ | $\frac{11}{V}$ | | $\frac{1111}{D}$ | $\frac{0}{V}$ | 10 | 2 | 2 | 3 |
| Lovett | 4 | $\frac{1111}{D}$ | $\frac{1111}{D}$ | $\frac{11}{V}$ | | $\frac{0}{V}$ | 10 | 2 | 2 | 2 — up |
| Slacks | 5 | $\frac{11}{V}$ | $\frac{1111}{D}$ | $\frac{1111}{D}$ | $\frac{1111}{D}$ | | | 1 | 3 | 5 |
| | 6 | | 10 | 13 | | | | | | |
| | etc | | | | | | | | | |

ORDER OF BOUTS

| 4 Fencers | 5 Fencers | | 6 Fencers | | 7 Fencers | | |
|-----------|-----------|-----|-----------|-----|-----------|-----|-----|
| 1–4 | 1–2 | 1–3 | 1–4 | 6–4 | 1–4 | 5–1 | 3–5 |
| 2–3 | 3–4 | 2–5 | 2–5 | 1–2 | 2–5 | 4–3 | 1–6 |
| 1–3 | 5–1 | 4–1 | 3–6 | 3–4 | 3–6 | 6–2 | 2–4 |
| 2–4 | 2–3 | 3–5 | 5–1 | 5–6 | 7–1 | 5–7 | 7–3 |
| 3–4 | 5–4 | 4–2 | 4–2 | 2–3 | 5–4 | 3–1 | 6–5 |
| 1–2 | | | 3–1 | 1–6 | 2–3 | 4–6 | 1–2 |
| | | | 6–2 | 4–5 | 6–7 | 7–2 | 4–7 |
| | | | 5–3 | | | | |

**Figure 38.** A completed fencing score sheet.

In case of a tie for second and third places, touches against each competitor (counted across boxes) are counted. The competitor with the least number of touches against her wins second place. In the event the number of touches against is the same for two or more competitors, the scorer counts touches for, by counting the number of touches in the competitor's vertical column.

In Figure 38, Dalton, Hewatt, and Lovett all had two V's and two D's, thus tying for second place. By counting across, it is determined that Hewatt and Lovett have an equal number of touches against them, but less than Dalton. Dalton automatically takes fourth place. Hewatt's vertical column (3) totals 10 touches "for," while Lovett's totals 13. The scorer has written the number of touches "for" and circled them in row 6 under the appropriate columns.

Thus, Lovett is awarded second place and Hewatt third place. If two fencers qualify from this pool for the final pool, Burdeshaw and Lovett would qualify. The scorer has written "Up" beside those competitor's rows, indicating that they have qualified to compete in the next round of the tournament. In the event a tie exists for first place, it is always fenced off in what is called a barrage, or fence-off. The winner is declared winner of the pool. First place is never determined by counting touches against opponents.

## TOURNAMENT ORGANIZATION

Fencing competitors, if they number more than eight, are placed into groups called pools. If some fencers are nationally classified, or are known to have more experience than others, they are ranked and separated into different pools. Depending upon how many pools exist and how much time is available for the tournament, the two top fencers from each pool graduate into a semifinal pool, from which the two or three top competitors are then placed in a final pool. The winners of this pool win the tournament. For example, if 32 women enter a tournament, they might be divided into four pools of eight fencers each. If three or four of the competitors are ranked, they would be separated so that each started in a different pool. The first four places from each pool would comprise two semifinal pools of eight each. Finally, the top four places from each of these might comprise the championship pool. Thus, if the winner of the tournament went undefeated, she might have won all 21 of her bouts — seven in each pool.

## JUDGING AND DIRECTING

Judging and directing fencing bouts are almost as much a part of learning to fence as learning the basic techniques. When small groups get together to fence informally, during class bouting, or especially during a fencing competition, you may be asked to judge or direct a bout. Learn the techniques of each of these officiating positions, and implement them conscientiously. Some fencers refuse to learn to officiate in either capacity, while others claim that they cannot adequately judge or direct and they therefore refuse to try. All fencers should be able to judge any level of fencing bout — no matter how advanced the fencers might be — and you should be able to direct any bout of fencers who are either less skilled or as skilled as you are. Of course, directing final pools in competitions will be the responsibility of advanced and experienced fencers, but there are many times when you will need to direct a bout.

There is also a very practical reason why you should understand the process of directing a fencing bout. Directing, as does judging, requires many subjective decisions. Directors, therefore, are as different as their personalities. As you fence, it is imperative that you understand how the director is "seeing" your attacks and defenses. You may think you are finding the blade with a light parry and making a quick riposte. One director may agree with you, but another may call your light parry an insufficient parry. If you understand the process of directing, you will understand his final decision regarding the technique and change your parry slightly. The director probably will not change the way he sees the bladework, so you must modify your parry slightly. It would be foolish for you to insist that your parry is sufficient and lose the bout. In a very real sense you must be sensitive to your director's behavior as well as your opponent's. For this reason alone, the ability to direct is an important skill to develop. Having the skill of directing also makes you a better contributor to a fencing club, class, or tournament.

## Judging

The essence of good judging is attentiveness and instant decision making. Position yourself, as the director puts the fencers on guard, approximately three feet behind and three feet to the side of one of the fencers (see Fig. 37). Be prepared to maintain this position throughout the bout. The fencers may move suddenly away from you, and you will find yourself running forward or backward in an effort to maintain your position. Stay in a constant state of readiness to move quickly, for it is embarrassing if you are caught out of position and you cannot vote on a touch.

Keep your eyes on the target of the fencer facing you. Do not hesitate to lean forward or sideward, to squat, or to make any other movement that is necessary for you to have an unobstructed view of the target. When the fencer beside you makes an action toward the target you are watching, make a decision instantly as to whether it hit. Your decision must be one of only four possibilities: (1) yes, it hit; (2) yes, it hit but was off-target; (3) no, it was not a good hit; or (4) abstain. If you see a hit or an off-target, raise your arm instantly in an obvious way so the director can see it. Abstain only if your vision is blocked by an arm or by the body of either fencer. Do not get in the habit of abstaining because you can't make a decision as to whether the point hit. Practice judging and force yourself to be decisive. If

you have an unobstructed view of the target and you know the
criteria of a good touch, then you should be able to say yes, yes—but
off-target, or no.

When you judge in a bout between good fencers, you will have
to make several decisions and store them until the director asks you
to vote. Several actions may occur within a very short period of time
and before the director can halt the bout. For instance, you may see a
beat-attack made toward the target you are watching, but it is
parried. You may see this beat-attack followed almost immediately
by a parry-riposte, and that followed immediately by another parry-
riposte which hits target. By the time the director stops the bout, you
have seen three actions toward the target you are watching: a beat-
attack which you decided was parried, a parry-riposte that you decided slid across the chest, and a parry-riposte which you decided
was good. You should be prepared to vote "No" on the first action,
"No" on the second, and "Yes" on the last action. Get in the habit of
mentally counting and deciding materiality on each action of a
phrase. As soon as the fencers end a phrase, if no hands were raised
and the director did not stop the bout, you may forget those actions
and begin your counting anew on the next phrase.

Judging is time-consuming and subjective, therefore electronic
scoring apparatus which eliminates the need for judges is used whenever possible. When it is not being used, you, as one of the judges,
can expedite matters if you make your decisions quickly, decisively,
and independently. Do not be influenced by the other judge who is
also looking at your target. The reason there are two judges watching
one target is so that independent votes from two different vantage
points may be obtained. You will defeat that purpose if you are
intimidated or influenced by the other judge.

### Directing

Although judges are eliminated when electric fencing equipment is used, the director is not. A need always exists for good
directors.

To direct a fencing bout you must have a sound knowledge of
the rules, some understanding and ability to recognize the basic
fencing skills, and the ability to make decisions. Inasmuch as these
requirements are also those necessary to be a good fencer, it is
logical for you to learn to direct as you learn to fence. Each ability
will enhance the other.

To direct a bout, position yourself far enough away from the strip
so that you can see both fencers in your field of vision. Focus your
eyes on the spot where their blades cross, and look between the
fencers most of the time. Your function is to recognize and be able to

reconstruct mentally each action of a phrase. Call a halt to the action as soon as you see a judge's hand raised. After you have called the halt, take whatever time is necessary for you to reconstruct the action, and then poll the judges who are behind the fencer who initiated the attack. The rules governing the establishment of right-of-way have already been discussed in the rules section.

You may need to describe the fencing phrase to the judges. For example, you may turn to them and say, "A single disengage attack was initiated from this side. Did it land?" If neither judge votes yes, you may turn to the other two judges and say, "The initial attack was parried, did the simple riposte from this side land?" If they both vote no, you may return to the other judges and say, "Did the second action toward the target—a parry riposte—land?" If they vote yes, award a touch against the competitor hit. If the judges disagree, poll them, add your own vote if you choose, and make your decision according to the rules (see page 71).

You will be more successful in your attempts to direct if you are quick to call a halt as soon as you see a judge's hand raised. Quickness in stopping a bout eliminates other fencing actions that may follow the hit to which the judge responded by raising his hand. If you can eliminate irrelevant actions that may confuse the judges, you can simplify your task. When you first begin directing, concentrate on a decision regarding which fencer has right-of-way. Decide who started the attack and whether it was direct or indirect. Secondly, decide whether it was parried. Third, decide whether the parry was executed properly and whether the riposte was immediate in following the parry. With practice, you will soon be able to do this much of the directing with ease. You might ask some of your friends to "set up" a fencing phrase of only three actions and let you try to recognize and reconstruct it. Study the rules, particularly those concerning right-of-way, and practice directing.

When you direct, firmly control the situation. Do not allow the fencers to talk while they are on the piste and do not let the judges attempt to reconstruct fencing actions. The judges should only answer your questions regarding materiality of hits. Do not get into discussions with them. If one judge of a pair raises his hand, poll him after you poll the other. You can be confident that he has a definite opinion, but you cannot be sure of the other judge. It is tempting for some judges, who might be unsure of an action, to agree with the judge who raised his hand. By polling first the judge who did not raise his hand, you can get an opinion that is uninfluenced by the other judge. If you have one judge you know to be more inexperienced and less effective than another judge, place the less skilled one so that he is watching the same side of the target that is facing you.

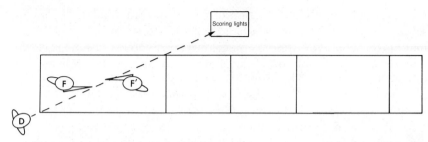

**Figure 39.**  Position of director in relation to electric scoring apparatus when fencers are at one end of the strip.

The electric scoring device simplifies your job, for you do not have ambiguity in terms of materiality. In addition, the scoring device is constructed so that if an off-target light and a hit light go on simultaneously on the same side, you know the off-target hit preceded the hit. You still have to make the same basic decisions regarding right-of-way. Your position for directing changes slightly, in that you have to keep the scoring apparatus lights within your vision as you watch the bladework. This position modification is greatest when the fencers are at extreme ends of the piste. In Figure 39 you can see the position of the director under these conditions.

Directing a fencing bout is challenging and enjoyable. Many people find a satisfaction in their ability to direct that is different from the satisfaction that they derive from fencing. Whether you enjoy it or not, you should have the experience of directing, for at most it gives you insights regarding your own technique, and at least it provides you with a basis for empathizing with the difficulties and responsibilities of the director.

## THE FENCER'S CODE OF ETHICS

The fencer's code of ethics includes unwritten rules of fencing that determine competitive behavior in both formal and informal bouts. The conscientious fencer will honor this code of ethics, whether he is fencing in his own home, a fencing salle, a fencing class room, or in a tournament.

1.  Be courteous at all times, displaying sportsmanship in formal and informal competition.

2.  Control your emotions and refrain from undue outbursts.

3.  Always salute your opponent before beginning a bout.

4.  Acknowledge, by a simple salute, a touch made by your opponent.

5.  The only statement you are allowed to make is the term "Ready." If you wish to stop the bout, you must stamp your front foot twice (appel).

6. In formal competition, if you do not understand why a touch was awarded against you, appel and politely request an explanation from the director. Do not argue with his decision.

7. Accept the judgment call of a judge regarding materiality of a hit. Do not try to intimidate or influence a judge.

8. When you watch a fencing bout, watch silently. It is unsportsmanlike to make noises or distracting movements while a fencing bout is underway.

9. Be gracious in fulfilling a request by competitors to judge or direct their bout.

10. When you have been eliminated from a tournament before the final pools have been fenced, offer to help score, time, judge, or direct some of the final bouts. Do not leave the premises the moment you have been eliminated from the tournament.

# CHAPTER 6

# STRATEGY

Techniques and rules discussed to this point are merely the tools that are used in implementing your strategy to defeat your opponent. The more carefully you have attended to your skill development, and the more accurate your techniques, the more attention you can give to the combination and order of presentation of the skills that make up your attacks and defenses. Actually, strategy is the essence of fencing. It is the system of techniques that you use to deceive your opponent and to protect yourself. All strategy is based upon a thorough analysis of your opponent, the techniques that you have at your disposal, and the decision of a plan of attack. For purposes of discussion, strategy is divided into offensive, defensive, bout, and tournament strategy.

## OFFENSIVE STRATEGY

Although a few fencers prefer to depend entirely upon their defensive game, "sitting back" in the on guard position waiting to riposte, almost all successful fencers find that good offensive attacking is necessary to their game. Before rushing into an attack with an opponent, however, it is necessary to have some idea of how you will attack and what kind of defense you are likely to see.

If you have already observed your opponent in competitive action, or if you have fenced him previously, then you have a pretty good idea of his strengths and weaknesses, his preferences, and his peculiarities. In this case, you can come into the bout with some established ideas of offensive strategy. You should have a "game plan" in mind, and stick to it as much as possible. If you have never observed nor fenced your opponent, you have a different problem. You must spend a few moments of the beginning of the bout attempting to analyze your opponent. What kind of parries does he use? Does he retreat every time he parries? Does he use the same type of parry each time? Does he prefer one line of defense over another? Does he continually fence out of distance?

To answer these questions, make a few feints in different lines. You might, for example, lightly beat your opponent's blade and extend your arm. This is a beat-feint. Does he fail to respond to your feint? If so, he may have a well established defense. Beat-feint emphatically in 4 line. Does he use a lateral parry 4 or does he counter parry 4? If he uses a lateral parry, try a beat-feint disengage. Does he follow your blade? If he does not parry your feint, try the same feint with a half-attack. Does he parry now? If he parries, does he follow it with a riposte? Is the riposte immediate or delayed? If it is immediate, is it coming back at you in the same line?

To test his reaction to having his blade controlled, place your middle blade against his foible and hold it there. Does your opponent let you keep contact? Does he draw his blade away? If he withdraws his blade, does he do so by changing lines or by retreating? If he changes lines by disengaging, disengage and place your blade against his foible again. Does he disengage again, in the same way, with the same tempo? Continue to analyze your opponent until you think you can predict his defense. Only then, should you attack.

Take the initiative, if possible, and control your opponent's movements rather than responding to his. Be aggressive. If your opponent retreats continuously, force him back to the end of the strip by attacking repeatedly. An opponent concerned about end line violations as well as his own defense is at a disadvantage.

A good offense is built upon your ability to predict your opponent's reaction to your initial thrusts. You can predict your opponent's response if you "condition" him or "set him up" for your final attack. To condition an opponent, repeat an attack several times until he becomes conditioned to parrying in that particular pattern. Following these conditioning attacks, change the attack very slightly and usually you can hit. For example, beat-attack in 4 line three times. Your opponent may be lulled into the parry 4 following the beat-attack. Begin your fourth attack in exactly the same way with the same rhythm but immediately following the beat, disengage. Usually you will find your opponent continuing his parry 4, just as you predicted. In summary, build a sequence of attacks in which the first ones are very similar, if not identical, and then follow with an attack that is just slightly different. This is a much more intelligent and effective approach than using several different attacks in a haphazard combination.

## DEFENSIVE STRATEGY

The best defensive strategy is to parry only when absolutely necessary. When forced to parry use as little movement as possible to complete the parry. Never parry if you do not have to, since your parry is a response which commits you to a given direction. Your opponent is trying, by feints and preparations on your blade, to make you move your bell guard out of position. He is trying to force you to parry and close one line, thus opening the other line. Obviously you can thwart him if you refuse to follow his thrusts. Of course, if his thrusts continue toward your target until they look as though they may land, a parry will be necessary. But make your parry small. The smaller your parry is, the quicker you can leave that position and get to another one. Fencers who parry wildly and take their points far out of line are easy prey to a fencer who feints well.

Alternate not only the type of parry you use but the times in which you use different parries. Use lateral parries, counter parries and compound parries (described in Chapter 7) alternately and in no predictable order. If your opponent disengages repeatedly, use lateral parries part of the time and counter parries part of the time. This technique makes it very difficult to predict your moves, and makes it harder for an opponent to plan any kind of systematic strategy.

If your opponent is a beginner or an aggressive fencer who feints wildly, letting his foil tip wander out of line, close the distance occasionally by stepping toward the attack while his point is out of line. This will nearly always render your opponent helpless with his point somewhere behind you; and if your point has preceded your closing, you may be rewarded by a touch against your opponent.

Keep your own foil tip pointing directly at your opponent's neck. Watch his target, not his foil tip. If you keep your eyes focused on his torso, you can note positions of foil, tip, and feet by using your peripheral vision. In addition, you can detect mannerisms that your opponent may have that are "tip-offs" that an attack is about to follow. Never let your guard drop, or your foil tip drop downward. Even if your opponent appears to be out of distance or uninterested in attacking, never let your arm drop down so that you are unprotected. Your opponent may suddenly make a high feint accompanied by a running attack, forcing you to violently and desperately return to the high parry position. If this is what your opponent has planned, he will simply deceive your vigorous parry and hit you in a low line.

If you discover that your opponent is perhaps a bit better than you are, and you have little confidence in your parries, accompany all of them with a retreat. If you have great agility, cautiousness, and a desire to win, sometimes these qualities will enable you to defeat a fencer who is slightly superior in technique.

## BOUT STRATEGY

You should have an overall bout strategy that includes decisions you have made regarding your offensive and defensive strategy. Use a variety of attacks and avoid using favorite ones repeatedly. If you find a particular type of feint is effective against your opponent, make a mental note of it and save it. You may need it for the last touch.

Above all, make your opponent fence your game, rather than letting him dictate the way you will fence. If you are generally aggressive and feel more comfortable making an attack, don't be forced into a defensive style. Instead, try to force your opponent out of his favorite fencing style. If he likes to attack, take the initiative with simple attacks and attack him first. If he likes to defend and touch with ripostes, wait him out. Refuse to attack until he does. You might also drive him back to the end line where he will be forced to attack or commit a line violation. If he likes to make preparations on your blade, keep your blade away from him so that he cannot find it. On the other hand, if he doesn't like preparations on his blade, then hold his blade with yours, pressure it, beat it, or do anything else to distract him.

Variety can be introduced into the bout by varying tempo and distance. If you have been attacking consistently and sequentially for the first part of the bout you might, if you are ahead in points, sit back for awhile. Or, if your attacks have been of one tempo, you might vary them in terms of speed.

An effective way to vary the bout, other than varying your timing, is to vary the distance at which you fence your opponent. Sometimes it is effective to fence out of distance—using quick advance lunges to make up the distance—after you have been fencing from a normal fencing measure. Other times it is effective to close the distance suddenly.

Be aware of the score of your bout, try to score first, and try to stay ahead. You can fence a waiting game if you are ahead, whereas you cannot if you are behind. When you are ahead in points, you have more alternative actions and you are free to experiment. Do not be afraid to use time to your advantage. If you are ahead in points and time is running out, remain on the defensive and wait. You know your opponent will have to come to you, and sometimes you can anticipate these attacks and finish the bout with a well-timed stop hit (see Chapter 7).

Above all, be patient and stay calm. Even if you get behind, be patient. When you get behind in points, you should try to concentrate on simple, exquisitely accurate, calculated attacks. Avoid panic and try to use strategy that was successful in the early part of the bout.

## TOURNAMENT STRATEGY

A competitive fencer usually has to fence many opponents within a single day, whether he is winning or losing. In large tournaments, as many as 15 or 20 opponents may be encountered. Also, large tournaments usually last for several hours. It is obvious that excellent physical conditioning is requisite to successful tournament experiences, but the winning fencer must also have the ability to prepare psychologically for each bout. Sometimes the differentiating factor between two highly skilled fencers is that one of them has the ability to maintain concentration and momentum through several bouts with intervening rest periods, whereas the other fencer does not. It is especially tempting to "let down" on a fencer you know to be a beginner or on one whom you've defeated in previous tournaments. This is careless behavior, however, and many times leads to a surprise victory for the beginner. A loss of this kind on the part of an experienced fencer can be so disconcerting that it can affect his fencing enough to lose other bouts. You should fence each fencer in the tournament with the same conviction, concentration, and seriousness.

Make it a practice to observe at least one bout of each of the competitors in the tournament. Study his weaknesses and strengths and try to establish a mental picture of his general strategy. At first this seems to be a monumental task, but if you compete frequently you will see a nucleus of the same competitors at each tournament and then strategy recognition becomes a matter of observing only a few newcomers at each tournament. Concentrate first on those fencers in your own pool, and if you get a few moments at the conclusion of your bouts you can observe fencers who were not in your qualifying pool. Remember that good competitors fence each individual with a different strategy, which is dependent upon his response. You cannot assume that a fencer whom you observe to be aggressive will be aggressive when he fences you, but the probability is high that he will be.

If you have some moves which work especially well for you, try to save them and use them only when you need points badly. Use the simplest moves you can to win. If you can win several bouts with simple disengages and coupés only, then competitors you fence later in the day will have little idea of other techniques that you might use. Your strategy will be an unknown quantity, and this is always disconcerting to competitors.

Maintain your equipment in good working order prior to the tournament, and keep it in a safe place during the tournament. You should never have to borrow equipment; most serious competitors have their foils functioning just as they want them. Should you break another's foil during competition, it can disrupt his competitive performance. Broken equipment is a nuisance when you have to interrupt a bout to exchange foils, for it disrupts the tempo of the bout and breaks up strategic sequences you may be constructing. Although equipment breakdowns cannot always be prevented, you should do your utmost to avoid them.

Check the recording of your scores intermittently throughout the tournament. Occasionally scoring errors occur and it is easier to catch them early in the tournament than after it is over.

Fencing tournaments can be extremely challenging, for you are faced with many different personalities and fencing styles within a relatively short period of time. Consider your first few tournaments as learning experiences and do not become discouraged if you are defeated several times. No amount of class or individual instruction can substitute for what can be learned in a tournament experience. Placing high in a good fencing tournament can be a most exhilarating experience, for it is tangible evidence that you have reached a culmination in that which is the essence of fencing—to hit without being hit, to win more bouts than you lose, and to do it all with the valor, the style, and the elegance that is the heritage of the sport.

## CHAPTER 7

# ADVANCED
# TECHNIQUES

Learning new attacks and defenses adds a new dimension to your strategy development. Advanced techniques and simple techniques complement each other; when advanced techniques are sprinkled into your strategy wisely, they make the simple attacks more effective. Keep in mind, however, that the objective in fencing is to touch your opponent. Be parsimonious: if you can touch with a simple attack there is no reason to use a complex one. Do not begin practicing advanced techniques if you have not mastered the simple ones. No matter how elaborate an attack may be, it will not be effective if it is poorly executed. Accurate timing is more important than strength, speed, or endurance.

Advanced techniques involve some slightly more aggressive footwork patterns, attacks with more complex timing requirements, defenses to protect against the more complex attacks, and some attacks that are "out-of-time" or without right-of-way.

## FOOTWORK

### Ballestra

The ballestra is a jump-lunge, and provides a method of springing unexpectedly at your opponent. It is an excellent technique for closing the distance rapidly. For this reason, short fencers usually master this footwork pattern. Because it has a rhythm of only two counts, it is faster than an advance-thrust-lunge which has a three count rhythm. The ballestra is accomplished by jumping forward with both feet. The feet strike the floor simultaneously; and as the rear foot makes contact, the rear leg immediately begins to extend to initiate the lunge. The foil arm, in order to obtain right-of-way, must reach full extension just prior to the lunge. If the lunge instantly follows the jump, the foil arm may be extended on the initiation of the jump. If the jump is prolonged, however, the foil arm may be extended just as the feet contact the floor on the jump. The jump should be forward, not upward. The feet do not leave the floor very far, but rather appear to be flying forward during the jump.

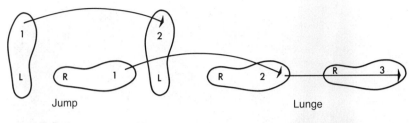

Jump

Lunge

Ballestra

**Figure 40.** Foot pattern of the ballestra.

### The flèche

The flèche is a running footwork pattern that is unique among fencing attacks in that the fencer does not return to the on guard position following the attack. Rather, following his attack the fencer runs past his opponent. The flèche should be used quite sparingly, as it depends upon the surprise element for success. Generally, because it is a surprise attack, the flèche consists of simple blade maneuvering. The flèche is easily parried if it is anticipated by your opponent, and this leaves you quite vulnerable since you can't parry easily while you are running. The flèche is a flashy attack; the fencer suddenly bursts forth in a flurry of blades and runs by his opponent. This usually draws exclamations from spectators. In addition, it gives one an unusually satisfying feeling to suddenly run all-out at your opponent and attempt to hit him as you pass. Do not be lured into inserting a flèche into almost every fencing phrase, however, or you will lose many bouts in a flashy manner.

You may execute a flèche in one of several ways, but however you do it remember that it is always preceded by a feint or an attack on the blade, and the foil tip must always precede the footwork. Almost simultaneously, extend your foil arm fully, shift your weight over your front foot and leap forward toward your opponent's target. Catch your weight following the leap by bringing your rear leg forward in front of your front one, and continue running past your opponent. A second method of initiating the flèche is to lunge, and then shift the weight while in the lunge over the front foot while continuing to reach toward the opponent with your blade. As the weight shifts over the front foot, spring toward your opponent by extending your front leg. Catch your weight by bringing the rear leg forward and continue running.

## Footwork Drills

Any simple attack may be preceded by a ballestra or a flèche. The best way to practice these footwork patterns is to repeat them

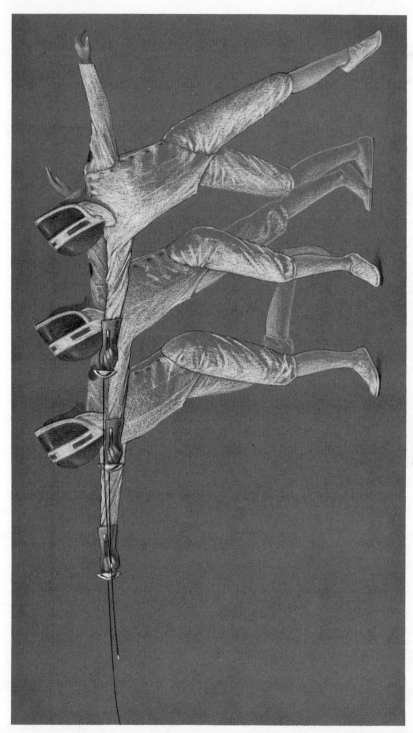

**Figure 41.**   The flèche; side view.

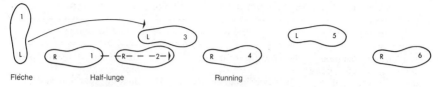

**Figure 41A.** Alternate foot pattern of the flèche.

with simple attacks until they are easily executed, and then practice alternating them with simpler footwork patterns. Below is an example sequence for the ballestra. After going through it, you may repeat the entire sequence using any of the simple attacks described earlier, and using the flèche pattern instead of the ballestra.

1. Practice the jump-lunge pattern alone.
2. Practice the ballestra with a straight lunge, simple attack in 4 line.
   a. Establish your correct measure against an opponent, so that you can easily hit from a straight lunge.
   b. Retreat once.
   c. Jump-lunge.
   d. Hit in 4 line.
   e. Repeat a, b, c, and d until your ballestra attack is smooth and flowing.
3. Precede a simple thrust-lunge by either the advance-lunge footwork pattern or the ballestra. Try to vary these two patterns so that your opponent cannot anticipate your moves.
4. Vary both the footwork pattern and direct or indirect attacks.

## ATTACKS

### The glisé

The glisé or glide attack is a sliding of your blade along your opponent's blade and into the target. This type of attack is usually a simple attack, in which the glisé is considered a preparation on the blade. Place the middle of your blade upon your opponent's foible. With a quick, deft movement apply slight pressure and slide your blade down your opponent's as you straighten your foil arm. Follow immediately with a lunge. This attack is also effectively combined with a disengage. The opponent generally will respond to the pressure and movement of the glide by a hurried lateral parry. As you detect the beginning of the parry, leave the glide and slip under the blade to hit in the other line. Your sudden departure from your opponent's closing parry will only serve to increase his lateral movement, thus increasing your chances of hitting.

**Table 10.** Common Errors in Advanced Footwork Techniques

| Error | Cause | Correction |
|---|---|---|
| 1. Inadequate distance covered when using the ballestra. | 1A. Jumping upward. | 1A. Jump forward; feet close to floor. |
| | 1B. Short lunge following jump. | 1B. Develop leg strength by resistance exercises, so that a forceful lunge can be initiated the instant the rear foot strikes the floor. |
| 2. Ballestra is too slow and cumbersome; so much time consumed in the footwork that attack is parried easily by opponent. | 2A. Jumping upward. | 2A. Jump forward. |
| | 2B. Ballestra is arrhythmic. | 2B. Strike the floor simultaneously with both feet, making one sound. The lunge is initiated as the rear foot strikes the floor, and is the second beat of a 2-beat rhythm. |
| 3. Flèche attack is parried easily. | 3A. Flèche is unwittingly tipped off so that opponent anticipates it. | 3A. Begin flèche from natural on guard position; use sparingly. |
| | 3B. Too much time between extension of arm and beginning of running pattern. | 3B. Initiate run immediately following thrust and body lean; develop strong legs so that if flèche is initiated from a lunge there is no time delay between extension and run. |
| | 3C. Excessive distance to be covered with flèche. | 3C. Initiate flèche from just slightly out of distance. |
| 4. Running into opponent's body and making contact. | 4A. Carelessness and poor control. | 4A. Exercise care and control. (This error is illegal and should be avoided; if the running pattern cannot be made without control, it should not be used until it has been practiced extensively.) |

## The pressure attack

The pressure attack is also a preparatory movement on your opponent's blade. Place your foible lightly against your opponent's middle blade. With a surprisingly sudden movement, apply moderate pressure against his blade. Generally, the opponent's response to your pressure will be a reflexive return of the pressure. Since you are anticipating this, you can drop your blade just prior to his return of the pressure. Inasmuch as your blade is no longer there, his pressure will carry his blade farther laterally than he anticipated and you may be able to slip under his blade and hit. On the other hand, he may respond even more violently in trying to return to his original line. If this is the case, you can disengage one more time and hit him in the line of the original pressure.

## The bind

The bind is an attack which may be used against an opponent who extends his foil arm toward you and maintains it there, or against a fencer who continually fences with a semistraight arm. Place your forte on top of his foible and move over your opponent's blade, pressing down as you bring your tip into contact with his low outside line. The secret to the bind is to dominate your opponent's blade by always using the strong part of your blade against the weak part of his. The movement from your 4 line over his blade is made only with the wrist, and the pressure against his blade and your arm extension to hit should be nearly simultaneous.

## Doublé

The doublé is an attack that may be used to take advantage of an opponent's habit of parrying only with a counter parry, particularly if your opponent uses a very large and circular counter parry. The doublé is really two disengages, both of which are made in the same direction. To doublé, disengage once, and as your opponent follows your blade around with his counter parry, you deceive his counter by disengaging again to hit. The doublé is simple in theory, but complex in its timing. You must make the initial disengage obvious in order to provoke the counter parry from your opponent. Your second disengage must be timed to your opponent's timing of the counter parry; as the counter parry is begun, slip under it by disengaging a second time and hit. Both disengages must be as small as possible, and your arm remains straight throughout the attack.

## Triple disengage

The triple disengage is a series of three disengages, usually executed against an opponent who uses only lateral parries and who fails to riposte. The triple disengage is initiated by disengaging to draw a lateral parry. When that parry is begun, disengage to the other line. As the parry changes, slip under and hit in the opening line. The triple disengage involves three movements and is therefore time-consuming. It is usually accompanied by an advance-lunge or ballestra against an opponent who retreats with his lateral parries. For instance, accompany the front foot movement of the advance with the first disengage, the rear foot movement of the advance with the second disengage, and follow with a lunge on the third disengage.

Inasmuch as the triple disengage consists of three distinct movements, it is easy to provoke a stop hit in the middle of it. It is, therefore, a somewhat dangerous attack to use indiscriminately. Unless you find an opponent who is particularly cooperative in consistently following your feints with lateral parries, you should not make a habit of using the triple disengage.

## Attack in second intention

The name of this attack describes it; it is a false attack, or a short attack followed by an attack off the riposte. The attacker does not intend to hit on the first attack, but is setting up the defender for the second attack. The rationale underlying this attack is that a defender is less able to protect himself on a second attack than he is on the first attack, since he may have erred slightly in his reaction to the first attack. This error might in turn evoke an overreaction to the second attack, thus enabling the attacker to hit on the second. Theoretically, if a defender's parry system is not flawless, he should become increasingly easier to hit on successive uninterrupted attacks. Additionally, the attacker is able to anticipate the action following the first attack, whereas the defender is not. This type of attack is particularly effective against a fencer who does not riposte effectively following his parries or one who repetitively and predictably uses the same riposte following his parries.

An example of an attack in second intention is a situation in which the attacker lunges with a simple attack into his opponent's 4 line, waits for the parry 4 and simple return riposte to his own 4 line, and then defends with parry 4 and attacks in second intention with a change riposte. The first attack, which is the false attack, may be executed so that it is somewhat short, and then the parry change-riposte is executed with a full lunge.

## Remise, redouble, reprise

In the event an opponent hesitates after a parry, fails to riposte, or escapes your touch by retreating without a riposte, you have the right to renew your attack. Three forms of renewal are the remise, redouble, and reprise.

REMISE.   The remise is a relatively simple attack in which a full lunge is made, but the blade is left in the line of attack rather than being withdrawn. This attack depends upon your opponent making the error of lunging with the body before he extends his arm on the riposte, or making a complex riposte rather slowly. You must keep in mind that the remise has no right-of-way, and it will not count unless it hits prior to your opponent's final action. If you notice that your opponent uses a very wide parry 4, for instance, and then lunges forward with the body well before the blade is extended, you might make a simple attack in 4 line. If it is parried, let your blade ride with the parry, and then as your opponent releases your blade return it immediately back to the closest target without bending your arm in the slightest or without leaning or recovering from your lunge. Your opponent will "run on to your blade," thus impaling himself. Remember, however, that if your opponent should parry properly and return immediately with a simple riposte executed properly, that you are hit and the touch will count against you.

REDOUBLEMENT. The redoublement is a renewed bladework that is made against an opponent who has parried but has not followed with a riposte or who has simply avoided your first attack by retreating. If you, in the first instance, stay in your lunge position and attack again; or if, in the second instance, you recover forward from the lunge and re-attack, you have redoubled.

REPRISE. The reprise is a renewed attack that is executed immediately after you have recovered to your on guard position. It may be in the form of an attack on the blade accompanied by the advance-lunge footwork pattern, or it may be initiated by a ballestra or flèche. Just as theatrical musicals many times have a reprise which is an abbreviated form of a previously presented song, so may a carefully calculated and fully developed fencing attack be modified slightly and repeated immediately as a reprise attack.

## Advanced Attack Drills

Advanced attacks should be practiced individually until they are automatic. After you have achieved technical skill in executing these

**Table 11.** Common Errors Made During Attacks in Second Intention

| Error | Cause | Correction |
|---|---|---|
| 1. Attack in second intention fails to evoke an initial parry riposte from opponent. | 1A. False attack is not believable. | 1A. Thrust your point deep enough toward your opponent to convince him that he should parry; a little body lean will drive the point closer. |
|  | 1B. Opponent is retreating and avoiding the riposte deliberately because he is anticipating the attack in second intention. | 1B. Use attacks in second intention sparingly or they lose their effectiveness. |
| 2. Making two actions out of the remise. | 2A. Bending the arm following your first arm extension. | 2A. Use the remise only when your attack is slightly short; i.e., once the extension and lunge have been made, leave the arm straight and the point in line. |

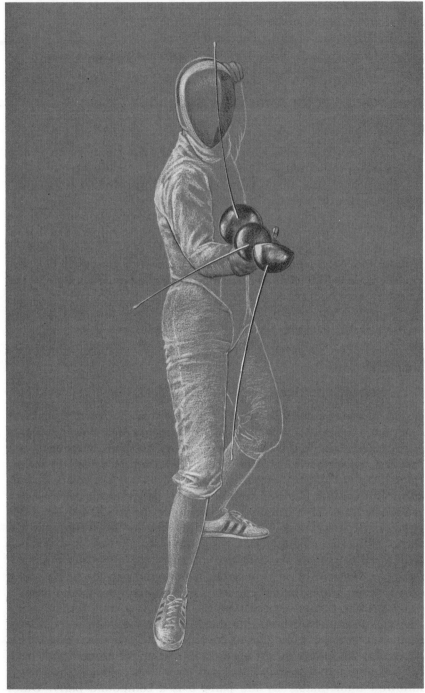

**Figure 42.** A compound parry: from parry 4 (foil raised) to parry 7 (foil lowered).

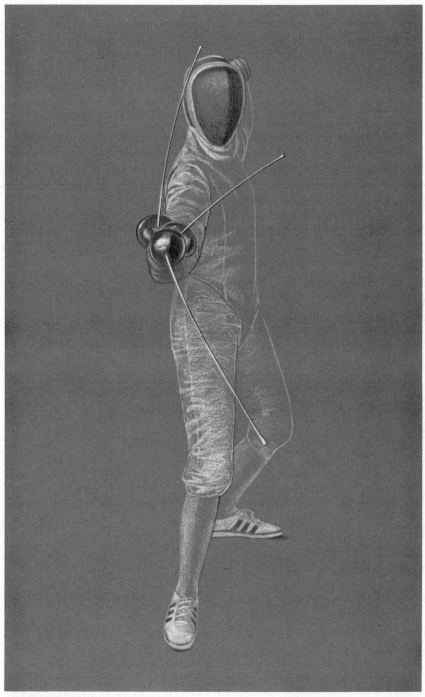

**Figure 43.** A compound parry: from parry 6 (foil raised) to parry 8 (foil lowered).

a high line parry to a low line parry. Because the tip of the foil, as it travels from one parry to the next, enscribes an arc in the air, these parries used to be called semicircular or half-counter parries. You would use a semicircular parry if you parried a feint in 6 line, discovered that your opponent had disengaged and was attacking your low 4 line, and you followed your parry 6 by cutting your blade into a parry 8 (see Figures 42 and 43).

COUNTER-LATERAL PARRIES. A counter-lateral parry is a counter parry followed by a lateral parry; i.e., a counter parry 4 followed by a parry 6. If, while executing a counter parry you fail to locate your opponent's blade, you sometimes can cut straight across your target with a lateral parry in the opposite direction of your counter and successfully defend yourself. If you fail to find your opponent's blade with a counter parry, it is obvious that your opponent is following your blade action in the same direction. A lateral parry is the best way to break up this type of attack. It is successful, for instance, against the doublé.

LATERAL-COUNTER PARRIES. It is also possible to follow a lateral parry with a counter parry. In the event you parry 4 but do not find the blade, and in addition you are not sure where the blade is, a counter parry of 4 in which your blade sweeps in a full circle across your target may find your opponent's blade. This type of parry is usually a desperation maneuver because you are already one action behind the attack and you don't know where your opponent's blade is. This parry is, therefore, generally accompanied by retreating and giving ground.

## Practice Drills for Advanced Defenses

In the left column below are attacks that your partner should make in order for you to practice the defenses in the right hand column. When you have completed practicing one of the defenses, change responsibilities so that your partner can practice the defenses.

| *Attack* | *Defense* |
|---|---|
| 1. Feint in high 6, disengage to attack in low 4. | 1. Semicircular parry from parry 6 to parry 8. |
| 2. Feint in high 4, disengage to attack in low 6. | 2. Semicircular parry from parry 4 to parry 7. |
| 3. Doublé from 4 to attempt a hit in 6. | 3. Counter parry 4, lateral parry 6. |
| 4. Doublé from 6 to attempt a hit in 4. | 4. Counter parry 6, lateral parry 4. |
| 5. Feint in 4, disengage to 6. | 5. Parry 4; if you miss the lateral parry 4, counter parry 4. |
| 6. Feint in 6, disengage to 4. | 6. Parry 6, if you miss the lateral parry 6, counter parry 6. |

**Table 13.** Common Errors Committed While Executing Advanced Parries

| Error | Cause | Correction |
|-------|-------|------------|
| 1. Difficulty in riposting following semicircular parries. | 1A. Allowing foil tip to wander too far away from target. | 1A. Keep foil tip pointed toward target as much as possible; when using semicircular parry, keep tip aimed no lower than the thighs of opponent. |
| 2. Being hit easily after having been deceived into making a semicircular parry. | 2A. Dropping forearm when making the parry. | 2A. Use only the wrist and fingers to execute the parry. |
| 3. Ineffectiveness of the counter-lateral or lateral-counter parries. | 3A. Large counter parries made by the entire forearm. | 3A. Make counter parries by small finger movements; think of making a "V" instead of a circle with the foil tip. |
|  | 3B. Allowing opponent to get so close that you don't have time to finish your lateral parry. | 3B. Retreat with the counter parry. |

# COMPOUND RIPOSTES

The compound riposte is one of the most effective techniques that a skillful fencer can develop. A compound riposte is any riposte that changes lines or has more than one action toward the target. Compound ripostes are extremely effective because they attack an opponent immediately after he has attacked, and he may not be prepared for an immediate complex return. Many good fencers develop a strategy in which they plan on hitting with a complex riposte rather than with the original attack. They use attacks in second intention—discussed earlier—almost exclusively; their first attacks are merely decoys to evoke parries and ripostes from their opponents. Their real intentions are to counter-riposte or to return their opponent's riposte with a compound one of their own.

### The change-riposte

The change-riposte is not technically a compound riposte; the foil tip and blade change lines but the action of the blade extension is all one action toward the target. The change-riposte is one of the most effective maneuvers you can learn, because it attacks the opponent in the line opposite to the one in which he has just attacked, forcing him to parry immediately after his attack in another line. In addition, if throughout the bout you interchange a simple direct parry riposte with a change-riposte, this interchange makes both types of riposte more effective. Your opponent may hesitate in his parry of your simple riposte because he can't be sure that you will stay in that line. His hesitation is all you need to enable you to hit with a simple quick direct riposte.

### Riposte with one or two disengages

Any riposte may be initiated as a feint followed by one or two disengages. Generally a riposte draws a parry since the defender is less in control following an attack than he is while sitting in the on guard position. You can use the fact that your riposte will probably evoke a spirited parry and, as that parry begins, slip under the blade to hit in the other line. This is a riposte with a feint-disengage. If the opponent recognizes the disengage and parries with a lateral parry, you may disengage a second time. In doing so you would have completed a double-disengage riposte.

### Riposte with a doublé

A doublé-riposte may be effective against an opponent who habitually follows his attacks with counter parries. As your opponent completes his attack, you parry. Follow this with your extension in the same line of attack. As his counter begins, follow the counter around with your foil tip and hit with a doublé in the other line.

## Practice Drills for Compound Ripostes

1. Following a series of straight attacks by your opponent by alternating the straight riposte with the change-riposte.
2. Alternate the change-riposte with the double-disengage riposte. See how many times out of 10 you can hit on the riposte.
3. Have your opponent follow 10 straight attacks by either a lateral parry or a counter parry. You attempt to hit with either a change-riposte if he uses a lateral parry, or by a doublé-riposte if he uses a counter parry.

## STOP HITS AND STOP HITS WITH OPPOSITION

A stop hit is a counterattack made on an attack. Two elements enhance its success: surprise, and the presence of an error made by

**Table 14.** Common Errors in Executing Advanced Ripostes

| Error | Cause | Correction |
|---|---|---|
| 1. Being parried when using a change-riposte. | 1A. Starting the disengage too soon. | 1A. Initiate the disengage only after your opponent starts his parry; he must have time to see your initial thrust in the line in which he first attacked. |
| 2. Hitting off-target on a change-riposte. | 2A. Leaning into the target, or starting the lunge too soon if opponent retreats with his parry. | 2A. Execute the change-riposte from the on guard position if possible; initiate the lunge only if the opponent retreats and then only after you have evoked the beginning of a parry and your arm is fully extended. |
| 3. Being parried after executing a doublé-riposte. | 3A. Disengages of doublé are too big and too slow. | 3A. Keep your parry in position; initiate the doublé directly from the parry; thrust straight toward the target and execute the disengages with the fingers only. |

the attacker. A stop hit is made by extending the arm suddenly in the face of a poorly executed attack, and by lunging if it is necessary to reach the target. The stop hit should be made just as the opponent lifts his forward foot to advance or to lunge. A safer way to make a stop hit is to extend your foil arm toward the nearest target area, leave your point in line, bring your rear foot up to the front foot, extend your legs, and remove your torso from the line of attack (see Fig. 44). If you assume this position quickly, your opponent will be unable to stop his attack and will "impale" himself on your point.

The stop hit will never work against a well-executed, simple attack; it is impossible to hit one full action ahead of a one-action attack. The stop hit is successful against fencers who use long, complicated attacks with several actions (especially poorly executed compound attacks), against fencers who advance within distance or who lunge with their body before extending their foil arm, and against short opponents.

In Figure 45 the fencer on the right has attacked with a bent arm while leading with his body. The fencer on the left has simply extended his foil arm and displaced his body as suggested in Figure 44.

Another type of stop hit is the 3-point stop hit in which the fencer drops his body suddenly as the attack is begun (see Fig. 46).

**Figure 44.** Body position for making a stop hit.

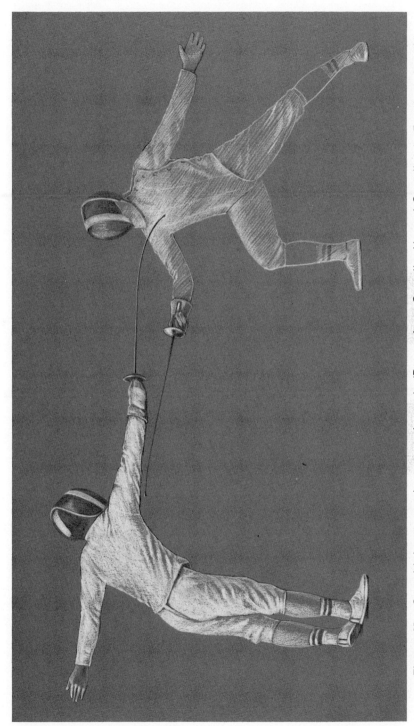

**Figure 45.** Stop hitting a poorly executed attack. (Drawn from Castello, H., and Castello, J.: Fencing. © 1960, The Ronald Press Company, New York.)

**Figure 46.** A 3-point stop hit.

**Figure 47.** A stop hit with opposition. (Drawn from Castello, H., and Castello, J.: Fencing. © 1960, The Ronald Press Company, New York.)

The weight is taken on the left hand for added support. This stop hit is rarely used, but would be effective if the attacker were poorly executing some type of compound coupé attack into your high line.

In a fencing phrase in which a stop hit is used, it is up to the director to decide whether the attacker had right-of-way or whether the stop hit was successful in beating the attack. It is obvious that the stop hit must be well timed and perfectly executed in order to be counted as a touch. It should be considered a high level skill that is to be practiced many times before it is attempted in a competitive bout. Above all, a stop hit should probably be used only once in two or three bouts. It is not a technique that a fencer should use habitually.

The stop hit becomes a stop hit with opposition when the extension of your blade is made with opposition against your opponent's blade, thereby closing the line simultaneously with your extension. In Figure 47 the fencer on the left has taken the attacker on the right by surprise by suddenly closing the line and extending his arm simultaneously. Sometimes the attacker will be so startled that he will reflexively withdrawn his attack, as has the attacker in Figure 47. Note his foil point in the air.

## Practice Drills for the Stop Hit and Stop Hit with Opposition

In the left column below are attacks that your partner should make in order for you to practice the defenses in the right hand column. When you have completed practicing one of the defenses,

**Table 15.**   Common Errors in Executing Stop Hits

| Error | Cause | Correction |
|---|---|---|
| 1. Missing a stop hit. | 1A. Bending the arm. | 1A. Extend the point and place all your concentration on aiming the point at the nearest target. |
|  | 1B. Jabbing at the target. | 1B. Let the opponent run onto your blade; you should not make a forward motion toward the target. |
| 2. Being hit as you make a stop hit. | 2A. Using the stop hit on a simple attack. | 2A. Use the stop hit only when you feel reasonably sure your opponent is going to make a compound attack. |
|  | 2B. Using the stop hit too frequently. | 2B. Use the stop hit sparingly, for it depends solely on surprise. |

change responsibilities so that your partner can practice the defenses.

| *Attack* | *Defense* |
|---|---|
| 1. Execute a double-disengage from 4 to 4 line. | 1. Stop hit as the first disengage is executed. |
| 2. Execute a double-disengage from 6 to 6 line. | 2. Stop hit as the first disengage is executed. |
| 3. Execute a coupé-disengage from 4 to 6 to 4. | 3. Stop hit as the first coupé is completed. |
| 4. Execute a triple disengage from 6 to 4 and 6 to 4; advance on the first disengage. | 4. Stop hit with opposition on the first disengage by stepping in and extending your arm and blade against your opponent's blade in 4 line. Make your step, close of line, and extension simultaneously. |

## CHAPTER 8

# FENCING WITH
# ELECTRIC EQUIPMENT

The electric foil and épée were born of necessity. The international juries at the Olympic level had degenerated into such squabbling and subjective argument that it was rumored the sport of fencing was about to be ejected from the Olympic games. Clearly, the need for an objective scoring device was critical. Thus, the electric foil, épée, and scoring device were conceived, and they have since revolutionized the sport of fencing with foil and épée. Electronic scoring has had a more dramatic impact upon épée because no right-of-way rule exists in épée. At any rate, the electric equipment and scoring device are becoming predominant in contemporary American fencing.

Almost all fencers who have more than a passing interest in fencing either own or experiment with electric fencing equipment. The requirement of electric equipment for entry into the majority of fencing tournaments, with the possible exception of high school and college intramural tournaments, has initiated a widespread use of electric equipment.

### Differences between conventional and electric fencing

The use of electric equipment not only changes the style and tempo of fencing tournaments, it changes the style and tempo of the sport of fencing. The electric weapon is heavier and differently weighted. The weight of a classical foil pommel balances the weight of the blade and the fencer is not required to use grip strength to maintain the proper blade position. The electric foil, however, is overall a heavier weapon, and the pommel cannot balance the weight of the electric point and taped foible. Thus, the fencer—especially a woman—is apt to grip the handle of the foil more tightly with the last three fingers. The result of this slight change of grip is to hold the foil in a somewhat more "broken line" position with the

**Figure 48.**   Gripping a pistol grip electric foil.

arm or to heavily strap, with a martingale, the grip into the hand and
wrist. Both alternatives increase the range of movement of the point
during the blade action, increase the striking force of the fencer,
increase the range of the parries, and diminish the old concept of
"conversation of the blades"—the hallmark of classical fencing. Wrist
and arm strength and endurance have become a factor, and women
especially should participate in exercises that will strengthen their
foil arm and hand. Many women use an Italian or pistol-grip electric
foil because of the additional gripping surfaces provided. Very few
women competitors at the national level use a French style electric
weapon.

The neophyte fencer should not be tempted to forego the disci-
Another major difference between electric and conventional fencing is the technique of making a touch. In conventional foil, a touch
is scored only if a judge *sees* the touch land and *decides* that it fulfills
the criteria of a good touch. It is imperative that a fencer make a
"nice clean touch" as well as leave the tip on the target at least long
enough for the judges to see it. Many fencers have had the experience of making a touch that was so quickly withdrawn that the
judge did not see it. The electric scoring device is not so particular.
All that is required is that the forward force of the weapon is great
enough (500+ grams) to depress the point for thousandths of a
second. Touches are now registered by the electric scoring device
that might be overlooked by the judges or, if seen, called passé or
flat. These factors have encouraged a more simplistic and vigorous
fencing style. The trend toward simplicity renders stop hits less
effective as an overall technique of attack. Extremely drawn-out
repartees with the blades, excessive compound attacks consisting of
several movements, and so called "tic-tac" parries in which the
opponents barely contact each others' blades, are now only an entry
in the records of fencing history.

The neophyte fencer should not be tempted to forego the disci-
pline of learning to properly execute the fundamentals of fencing as
enumerated in Chapters 3 and 6, however. The fundamental con-
cepts of foil fencing are still true. The smaller bladework you use,
the more difficult it is for your opponent to see it. The smaller your

parries, the quicker you can return the riposte. The electric scoring device will still not be activated by force upon the side of the point (flat touch). Mastery of the fundamentals will reward you with ultimate success in electric fencing as well as in conventional fencing. This mastery is just a little more difficult to accomplish when using electric equipment, and it is tempting to become a "hacker." To keep your fundamentals intact, continue to practice basic skills with conventional foil as well as with the electric foil.

## ELECTRIC EQUIPMENT

The three additional pieces of equipment that you must purchase are a metallic lamé vest, an electric body cord, and an electric foil. The metallic vest is made of a wire mesh layer on the outside and a plastic insulating lining on the inside. It covers only valid target area and is worn over your regular white cotton jacket.

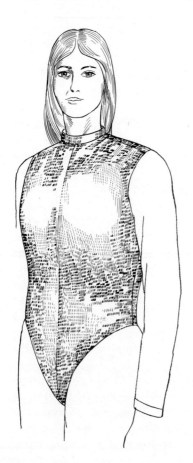

**Figure 49.** Metallic lamé vest.

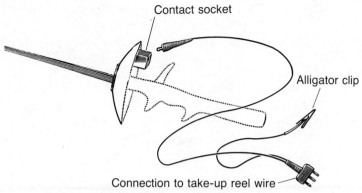

Contact socket

Alligator clip

Connection to take-up reel wire

**Figure 50.**   Insulated electric body cord.

The body cord connects your foil to a reel wire which goes to the electric scoring apparatus. The cord, attached to a socket in the electric foil bell guard, runs up the sleeve of your cotton jacket, down your back, and plugs into the reel wire. An alligator clip fastened to your jacket serves as a ground contact and also helps take the pull off the reel wire. As you advance toward your opponent's end of the strip, the reel wire "pays out" of the reel that is bracketed to the floor beyond the run-back room at the end of the strip. As you retreat toward the reel, it "takes up" excess reel wire.

### The scoring device

The electric foil and scoring device complete an electric circuit except when the foil tip is depressed with sufficient force. The

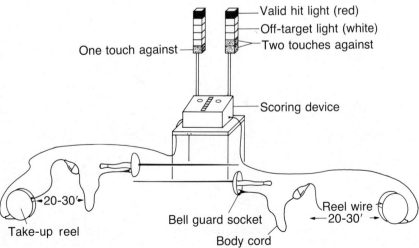

Valid hit light (red)
Off-target light (white)
One touch against
Two touches against
Scoring device
20-30'
Reel wire
20-30'
Take-up reel
Bell guard socket
Body cord

**Figure 51.**   Electric scoring apparatus.

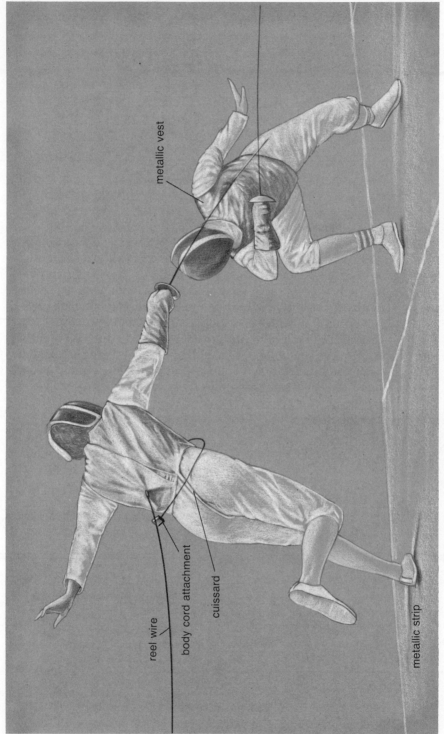

**Figure 52.** Use of electric fencing equipment in a tournament bout.

metallic vest

reel wire

body cord attachment

cuissard

metallic strip

circuit is then interrupted, and a signal — depending upon the type of interruption — is sent. If the tip hits the opponent's body somewhere other than on his metallic vest, the electric scoring device will flash a white light indicating that the touch was off-target. If the tip hits anything that is electrically grounded, such as your opponent's foil or the metallic mesh strip, the scoring device is not activated and no lights flash. A hit against an uncovered wooden or rubber floor will register as an off-target hit; thus, ground judges are used in tournaments where strips are not covered with metallic mesh.

If your foil tip is depressed against your opponent's metallic vest, a colored light is flashed on the scoring device. The device is built so that an off-target white light will not turn on if a valid touch first occurs on the same side. Conversely, if the white off-target light flashes simultaneously with the colored valid-touch light, the director knows that the off-target came first.

The scoring device has two columns of lights, one column containing seven lights for each fencer. A competitor has, serially from top to bottom, a green or red valid-hit light, a white off-target light, and five lights which are activated one at a time as a fencer has touches awarded against him. The five lights are lighted by the scorer so that both fencers and spectators can keep up with the score of the bout.

### Advantages and disadvantages of electric fencing

Electric fencing provides the advantage of speeding up the bouts because the scoring device eliminates the need for juries and their consequent polling and deliberating time. In addition, it eliminates much of the doubt and subjectivity of determining materiality of touches. A few disadvantages accompany the use of electric equipment. One, previously mentioned, is that the objectivity of the scoring apparatus and the heaviness of the electric weapon have deemphasized classic fencing form and resulted in a loss of some of the grace, beauty, and charm of the sport. Other disadvantates are that electric equipment is more expensive and electrical breakdowns are more frequent than conventional foil breakdowns. It is almost imperative to own two electric foils and two body cords, to ensure at least one operative set. Electric equipment must be consistently checked and immaculately cared for.

In spite of the disadvantages, most fencers prefer electric equipment. The loss of the old charm of fencing has been more than compensated for by the evolution of a new athletic and exciting style of fencing. Electrical fencing is really a different experience; and if you have the opportunity to fence electrically, you should try it.

## CHAPTER 9

# SELF TESTING

The most rewarding evidence of progressing fencing ability is, of course, to see yourself beginning to score touches on opponents who used to be difficult to hit. It is, however, also helpful to have a way of measuring your progress in terms of form and objective scoring techniques. This chapter includes several evaluations that you may use to determine your progress in learning fencing skills. In order to test yourself on most skills you will need a partner. It is impossible to learn to fence by yourself, as is implied by the fact that most of the practice drills suggested in this book require the use of a partner. As you learn to fence with a partner, the two of you can also evaluate each other.

## BASIC FORM AND FOOTWORK RATING SCALE

Have your partner place a check in the space provided by the description of each skill. Add all the checks and enter the total. The following evaluations describe possible totals:

| | |
|---|---|
| Excellent | 21-23 |
| Good | 17-20 |
| Average | 12-16 |
| Practice | -11 |

I. On Guard
    A. *Foil arm*
_____ 1. Elbow approximately 6 inches away from body
_____ 2. Pommel flat against wrist
_____ 3. Hand supinated
_____ 4. Foil and arm continuous, an unbroken line
_____ 5. Point in line with opponent's neck

B. *Non-foil arm*
_____ 6. Upper arm parallel with floor
_____ 7. Forearm at right angles with upper arm
_____ 8. Hand relaxed, approximately at right angles with forearm
C. *Torso*
_____ 9. Right shoulder profile shown to opponent (left shoulder if left-handed)
_____10. Torso erect
_____11. Hips tucked under
D. *Legs*
_____12. Feet at right angles
_____13. Feet approximately two of your own foot lengths apart
_____14. Right knee and foot pointed toward opponent
II. Footwork
A. *Advance and Retreat*
_____15. Torso position of on guard maintained throughout ad-
vance
_____16. Right foot moves first if advancing; left foot moves
first if retreating
_____17. Both feet stay close to the floor, but do not slide.
B. *Lunge*
_____18. Foil arm and blade extend prior to body movement
_____19. Non-foil arm extends behind body
_____20. Right foot stays close to floor; points directly at oppo-
nent
_____21. Right knee is directly over right instep at full lunge
_____22. Major power generated from rear leg
_____23. Rear leg is fully extended, with foot flat on floor

## DYNAMIC SKILL TEST

The following tests of your skill may be scored to give you an evaulation of your performance level in the dynamic or moving skills of fencing. Use the test form supplied at the end of this chapter to determine your overall progress in learning fencing skills.

### Hitting accuracy

_____ 1. Place a 2 inch square of adhesive tape on the wall. From an on guard position at the correct fencing distance away from the wall, lunge 10 times. Record the number of times you hit the tape.
_____ 2. From an on guard position approximately 10 feet away from the wall target, advance-thrust-lunge 10 times. Record the number of times you hit the target.

_____ 3. Place a 2 inch square of tape on your partner's jacket in approximately a high line position. Start 10 feet away and, using the ballestra, attack 5 times in 4 line and 5 times in 6 line. Your partner should open the line in which you are aiming; he should not parry your attempts. Record the number of hits.

## Bladework

_____ 4. Stand in the on guard position close enough to your partner so that you can hit with only an extension of your arm. Your partner contacts your blade with his. With no warning, he should apply moderate quick pressure to your blade. As you feel the pressure, disengage and hit the target in the other line. Execute 5 with pressure applied against your blade in 4 line, and 5 with the pressure applied in 6 line. Record the number of hits.

_____ 5. Determine how many times out of 5 attempts you can beat-disengage successfully when your beat is preceded by a beat-attack. To do this, use the beat-attack as many times consecutively as you wish. Do not count them, for they are your preparations preceding your attack. Once you attempt the beat-disengage, however, you must count it as one trial.

_____ 6. Determine the number of times out of 5 you can hit with a coupé-disengage when your attack is preceded by a coupé. Use the conditioning procedure outlined in 5, only alternate the coupé with the coupé-disengage.

_____ 7. Determine the number of times out of 5 you can hit with a doublé disengage when your attack is preceded by a single disengage. Use the conditioning procedure outlined in 5, only alternate the single and double disengage.

_____ 8. Determine the number of times out of 5 you can hit with a doublé when your attack is preceded by a disengage. For this test item, your partner must parry all attacks with a counter parry.

## Parries

_____ 9. Have your partner attack you 10 times, using either a straight attack, a beat-attack, or a disengage. These attacks should be rotated randomly. Record the number of attacks you successfully parried.

_____10. Defend yourself against 10 of your partner's randomly rotated attacks from the following: beat-disengage, coupé, coupé-disengage. Record the number of successful parries.

_____11. Defend yourself by using parry 7 or 8 against 5 attacks in low 4 and 5 attacks in low 6. Record the number of successful parries.

_____12. Defend yourself by using counter parries against 5 disengages from 4 to 6, and 5 disengages from 6 to 4. These attacks should be randomly rotated. Record the number of successful parries.

_____13. Defend yourself by counter parries against 5 disengages from 4 to 6 line, and 5 disengages from 6 to 4. The difference in this item from 12 is that your attacker will liberally sprinkle straight attacks, forcing lateral parries from you, in between his disengage attacks. Record the number of successful parries. (If you can execute a successful counter parry against ten disengages that are interspersed among straight attacks, you are progressing very well.)

## Riposte

_____14. Have your partner attack you 10 times, using a straight attack, a beat-attack, or a disengage. Record the number of times you hit with a single riposte from a lateral parry. Your partner should not parry your riposte.

_____15. Same as above, only your partner attempts to parry your riposte.

_____16. Your partner attacks with a straight attack. Record the number of times out of 10 attempts you can hit with a double-disengage riposte. You may follow some of your parries with a single riposte or a change-riposte in order to deceive your attacker. These straight ripostes will not count as trials. Your partner should attempt to parry your change-riposte.

_____17. Your partner attacks with a straight attack. Record the number of times out of 10 attempts you can hit with a double-disengage riposte. You may follow some of your parries with a single riposte or a change-riposte in order to deceive your attacker. The simple, and change-ripostes will not count as trials. Your partner should attempt to parry all your ripostes.

### Simulated competition

_____18. Record the number of times out of 10 attacks you can hit your partner. Use any attack, and he can use any defense.

_____19. Have your partner attack you 10 times. Record the number of successful defenses you make.

_____20. Have your partner attack you 10 times. Record the number of hits you make with a riposte. Your partner can use any attack, and you may use any parry riposte combination.

## FENCING SKILLS RATING SCALE

| Basic Form and Footwork | | | Dynamic Skills Test | | | |
|---|---|---|---|---|---|---|
| | Possible Score | Achieved Score | | | Possible Score | Achieved Score |
| I. On Guard | | | Hitting | | | |
| A. Foil arm (1–5) | 5 | _____ | accuracy | 1. | 10 | _____ |
| B. Non-foil (6–8) | 3 | _____ | | 2. | 10 | _____ |
| arm | | | | 3. | 10 | _____ |
| C. Torso (9–11) | 3 | _____ | Bladework | 4. | 10 | _____ |
| D. Legs (12–17) | 6 | _____ | | 5. | 5 | _____ |
| | | | | 6. | 5 | _____ |
| II. Footwork | | | | 7. | 5 | _____ |
| A. Advance- | | | | 8. | 5 | _____ |
| retreat (15–17) | 3 | _____ | Parries | 9. | 10 | _____ |
| B. Lunge (18–23) | 6 | _____ | | 10. | 10 | _____ |
| | | | | 11. | 10 | _____ |
| Subtotal | 26 | _____ | | 12. | 10 | _____ |
| | | | | 13. | 10 | _____ |
| | | | Riposte | 14. | 10 | _____ |
| **Total Evaluation** | | | | 15. | 10 | _____ |
| | | | | 16. | 10 | _____ |
| Basic footwork achieved score _____ | | | | 17. | 10 | _____ |
| | | | Simulated | 18. | 10 | _____ |
| Dynamic skills achieved score _____ | | | competition | 19. | 10 | _____ |
| | | | | 20. | 10 | _____ |
| Evaluation: | | | | | | |
| | | | Subtotal | | 180 | _____ |
| Excellent | 182 + | | | | | |
| Good | 162 − 181 | | | | | |
| Fair | 142 − 161 | | | | | |
| Practice harder | ⩽141 | | | | | |

## ANALYSIS OF COMPETITIVE EFFICIENCY

Below is a chart which, if completed periodically, will give you direction in which skills you should practice. Referral to this chart every three months will also give you some idea as to how you are progressing in terms of competition.

| | Attempted but unsuccessful in informal bouts | Successful in informal bouts | Attempted but unsuccessful in competition | Successful in competitive bouts |
|---|---|---|---|---|
| ATTACKS | | | | |
| Straight thrust | | | | |
| Disengage | | | | |
| Coupé | | | | |
| Beat-attack | | | | |
| Feint-disengage | | | | |
| Beat-disengage | | | | |
| Double-disengage | | | | |
| Coupé-disengage | | | | |
| Glisé | | | | |
| Pressure-preparation | | | | |
| Bind | | | | |
| Doublé | | | | |
| Triple disengage | | | | |
| Remise | | | | |
| DEFENSE | | | | |
| Parry 4 & 6 | | | | |
| Parry 7 & 8 | | | | |
| Semicircular parry | | | | |
| Counter parry | | | | |
| Lateral-counter parry | | | | |
| RIPOSTE | | | | |
| Simple | | | | |
| Indirect | | | | |
| Doublé-disengage | | | | |
| Doublé | | | | |
| ATTACKS OUT-OF-TIME | | | | |
| Stop hit | | | | |
| Hit | | | | |

## CHAPTER 10

# TERMINOLOGY

Many names and phrases that are used in fencing have several synonyms. Much of the duplication is due to the fact that fencing originated in Europe and many French and Italian terms have remained in the argot of the fencer. Inasmuch as French is the international fencing language, many fencers enjoy retaining French terminology. In the event two or more terms are used frequently they will be separated by semicolons and listed below. The pronunciation is provided in parentheses. When terms are pronounced as in English, pronunciation is not provided.

| | |
|---|---|
| *Appel* (ah-pell'); *Call* | Stamping the forward foot twice in order to request that fencing action be temporarily ceased. |
| *Attack in second intention* | A false, sometimes short, attack that has as its purpose not a hit, but the provocation of a parry-riposte which the attacker intends to parry and follow with a scoring counter-riposte. |
| *Attack on preparation* | Initiating an attack just moments before the opponent begins an attack; i.e., while the opponent is applying pressure to the blade, beating, feinting, or doing any movement other than a movement initiated toward the target. This type of attack is particularly effective when opponents have a revealing mannerism that always precedes their attack. |

| | |
|---|---|
| *Ballestra* (bah-les' tra); *Jump-lunge* | A footwork pattern designed to cover considerable distance in a short period of time. It is a jump followed by a lunge as the rear foot contacts the floor. |
| *Barrage* (bar-rahzg'); *Fence-off* | A bout fenced to break a tie for a qualifying position in a fencing tournament. It is possible to have a three-way barrage in the event three fencers are tied for one position. |
| *Bind; Liement* (lay-monh') | An aggressive action in which the attacker removes a blade by enveloping it with his own and pressuring it from a high line to a low line. |
| *Closed line* | A line which is protected by the arm and bell guard. |
| *Compound attack; Composed* | Any attack which includes more than one action. |
| *Corps à corps* (core-ah-core); *Clinch* | A stalemate in which two fencers' guards or blades are locked and neither will retreat. |
| *Counterattack* | An attack made on an attack; a stop hit, or a time-hit, if it is made while closing the line in which the attack is being made. |
| *Coupé* (coo-pay'); *Cut-over* | An attack in which the blade is sliced sharply over the opponent's just prior to the forward thrust. |
| *Derobement* (dee-robe'ment); *Deception* | Evasion of an opponent's attempt to deflect or bind the blade. |
| *Doublé* (doo-blay'); *Double* | A compound attack in which the attacker disengages to draw a counter parry, and then evades the counter parry. It is a full circle and a half. |

| | |
|---|---|
| *Envelopment* | Circling the opponent's blade from one line to the other and back to the original line. |
| *Feint* | Extending the arm toward the target in order to draw a parry. Used to determine what parry an opponent may use. |
| *Fencing measure* | The distance that is maintained between two fencers throughout a bout. |
| *Fencing time; Temps d'escrime* (tohn-day-skrim′) | The time required to perform a single fencing action. |
| *Flèche* (flesh) | A running attack that is initiated while out of the normal fencing measure; many times accompanied by an attack on the blade. The term fléche is the French term for arrow. |
| *Forte* (fort) | Portion of blade near the bell guard. |
| *Glide; Coulé* (coo-lay′); *Glisé* (glis-ay′) | A sliding of the blade along the opponent's blade prior to an attack. Many times it is accompanied by a sudden change of tempo. |
| *Martingale* | A wrist strap used to hold the foil grip next to the wrist. |
| *Passé* (pah-say′); *Slide* | A nondirect hit; the tip of the foil slides across the target rather than being the culminating penetration of a direct thrust. |
| *Phrase d'armes* (phrase-darms′) | A sequence of fencing actions that is unbroken by a pause; when there is a lull, or one fencer retreats, the phrase is completed. |
| *Pressure* | Applying pressure to the opponent's blade to entice him into |

overreacting. The overreaction may thus be evaded and an attack initiated while the opponent is on the defensive.

*Redouble; Replacement*

A renewed attack against an opponent who consistently parries without riposting.

*Remise* (ree-meeze'); *Insistence*

Leaving the point in line at the conclusion of an attack that falls short and letting the opponent run on to the blade. This is particularly effective when an opponent moves forward before he extends his arm on a riposte.

*Reprise* (ree-preeze')

Retaking an attack; reinitiating an attack immediately following a return to the on guard position.

*Salle d'armes* (sahl-darms')

A fencing club or room used to instruct in the weapons of fencing; foil, épée, and saber.

*Time-thrust*

An attack made on an attack, in which the line is closed and the riposte is made all in one motion.

# BIBLIOGRAPHY

## BOOKS

Castello, Hugo, and Castello, James.: *Fencing.* New York, Ronald Press, 1962. One of the classic books on the subject of fencing, written by two sons of one of the foremost fencing masters in this country. The book has excellent remarks on competitive strategy and has one of the best chapters on electrical foil fencing. Particularly good is their discussion of trouble-shooting in the event that electrical equipment breaks down.

Crosnier, Roger.: *Fencing with the Electrical Foil.* New York, A. S. Barnes and Company, 1961. A book that is helpful to those interested in tournament competition. A comprehensive discussion of selection, maintenance, and use of electric fencing equipment.

Palffy-Alpar, Julius.: *Sword and Masque.* Philadelphia, F. A. Davis Company, 1967. An interesting and unique contribution to fencing publications. Contains one of the most comprehensive chapters available on the history of fencing. Also includes an interesting chapter on stage fencing and combat with unusual fencing weapons such as the mace and chain. Excellent photographs.

Sports Illustrated: *Sports Illustrated Book of Fencing.* New York, J. B. Lippincott Company, 1961. A bound copy of the fencing articles that have appear in *Sports Illustrated.* Figures and illustrations of fencing technique are unusually good.

Vince, Joseph. *Fencing.* New York, Ronald Press Company, 1962. Good coverage of all three weapons—foil, épée, and saber. Includes list of typical fencing drills with which one may practice skills. Representative of the West Coast fencing philosophy.

## RULE BOOKS

American Association for Health, Physical Education, and Recreation: *Fencing-Bowling Guide.* Washington, American Association for Health, Physical Education, and Recreation. A rule book for girls' competition in fencing containing many articles about various phases of the game. Published every two years. 1921 16th Street, N.W., Washington, D.C. 20036.

Amateur Fencer's League of America: *Fencing Rules and Manual.* West New York, New Jersey, Amateur Fencer's League of America. Contains rules for competitions and organization of competitions. Also contains administrative procedures of the AFLA and lists Olympic, Pan-American, and World Champions in fencing. 33-62nd St., West New York, New Jersey, 07093.

National Collegiate Athletic Association: *The Official Fencing Guide.* New York, National Collegiate Athletic Association. Official college and school boy rule book in America. Published annually with any new rules or rule changes included. Has college records and lists qualified fencing officials in the United States. College Athletic Publishing Service, 349 East Thomas Road, Phoenix, Arizona, 85012.

## MAGAZINES

Amateur Fencer's League of America: *American Fencing.* West New York, New Jersey, 07093. A bi-monthly publication. This magazine is designed for members of the AFLA. It contains articles regarding contemporary problems in directing, team selection, or teaching techniques. It has several reports on European fencing and editorials comparing American fencing with fencing in other parts of the world. It also contains reports of fencing activities in the various sections of the country.

National Fencing Coaches Association: *Swordmaster*. Madison, Wisconsin, 16 North Carrol St. A magazine that is issued quarterly to members of the NFCA. It is designed to aid fencing teachers and coaches by publishing articles on coaching, teaching, and fencing techniques.

## MAGAZINE ARTICLES

"Art of the duel." Essay from his translation of Pushkin's Eugene Oregin. *Esquire*, *60*:54–55. July, 1963.

Cheatum, Billie Ann. "Benefit of the Doubt." Division for Girls and Women's Sports, Bowling-Fencing-Golf Guide, 1960-1962. Washington, American Association for Health, Physical Education, and Recreation. 1201 16th Street, N.W., Washington, D.C. 20036.

McBride, Joe. "How to Watch a Fencing Match." *The Scholastic*. A Notre Dame publication. February 8, 1957, pp. 27-33.

"Simple Touché Indicator for Fencers." *Electric World*, *64*:48. August, 1960.

Wortman, L. A. "Fencing with Electrical Foils." Division for Girls and Women's Sports, Bowling-Fencing-Golf Guide, 1960-1962. Washington, American Association for Health, Physical Education, and Recreation. 1201 16th Street, N.W., Washington, D.C. 20036.

## FILMS

*Beginning Fencing*. 35mm foil film strips in color with sound recordings by Maxwell Garret. Covers offense, defense, strategy, and tactics. Related information available in "How to Improve Your Fencing" and "Fencing Instructors Guide." Purchase or rent from The Athletic Institute, 805 Merchandise Mart, Chicago, Illinois, 60654.

*Techniques of Foil Fencing*. 16mm black and white film in which Helene Mayer, former Women's World Champion, demonstrates. Fencing techniques in normal and slow motion close-up shots are a special feature. Purchase or rent from: The University of California, Extension Film Center, 2223 Fulton St., Berkeley, California, 04720.

*Fencing—1964 Olympics—Tokyo*. 16 mm black and white film explaining training and competitive techniques of the world's outstanding fencers. Compete bouts are featured. Rental only from Amateur Fencer's League of America, 33-62nd St., West New York, N.J. 07093.

*Omnibus*. 16mm black and white sound film. Excellent film to explain fencing to the neophyte or non-fencer. Superb cinematography. Purchase or rent from Amateur Fencer's League of America, 33-62nd St., West New York, N.J. 07093.

*Instructional Foil*. 16mm black and white film by Professor J. Martinez Costello. This film records a lesson progressing through foil fundamentals. Slow motion and close-ups are used; titles facilitate the recognition of attacks and parries. Purchase or rent from Castello Fencing Equipment Company, 30 East 10 St., New York, N.Y. 10003.

*Foil Fundamentals*. 16mm black and white film; descriptive titles by Professor George Santelli. Presents formal salute, on guard position, footwork, attacks, and defenses. Purchase or rent from Amateur Fencer's League of America, 33-62nd St., West New York, New Jersey, 07093.